Introduction to the
Scottish Children's Panel

Alistair Kelly as Fife's Regional Reporter was until his retirement in 1996 Scotland's longest serving full-time children's reporter. He has an expert and longstanding knowledge of the Scottish Children's Panel and is sensitive to the problems presented by children drawn to public attention. As well as outlining the system, this book includes his own suggestions for reform to meet international standards.

Introduction to the

Scottish Children's Panel

Alistair Kelly

WATERSIDE PRESS
WINCHESTER

Introduction to the
Scottish Children's Panel

Published 1996 by
WATERSIDE PRESS
Domum Road
Winchester SO23 9NN
Telephone or Fax 01962 855567
E-mail INTERNET:106025.1020@compuserve.com

ISBN Paperback 1 872870 38 4

Cataloguing-in-publication data A catalogue record for this book can be obtained from the British Library

Cover design by John Good Holbrook Ltd, Coventry

Printing and binding by Antony Rowe Ltd, Chippenham

To my wife Joyce, children Graeme and Alison

and my grandchildren Craig, Jane and Calum

Preface

The Scottish children's panel is unique in its welfare approach to the difficult problems presented by children in trouble drawn to public attention. The children's panel system is described from an understanding of the concept of the local community taking responsibility for children in trouble in their midst, applying effectively a philosophy of care. Unfortunately that philosophy of care has been somewhat diluted by the Children (Scotland) Act 1995 in response to the two inquiries of Orkney and Fife (1992) and the tragedy of the South Ayrshire case (1995). This welfare justice approach has to be judged taking into consideration the provisions of the European Convention on Human Rights (1987) and the United Nations Convention on the Rights of the Child (1989) as demanding a proper respect for children's rights in accordance with international standards.

The purpose of this book is to describe in plain language the Scottish children's panel system, its philosophy of care and to advocate radical reform of the system taking into account the 1995 Act and the demand for a proper respect of children's rights in Scotland within the European context.

Alistair Kelly
Fife, Scotland
May 1996

Introduction to the
Scottish Children's Panel

Alistair Kelly

CONTENTS

8 Voluntary and Compulsory Supervision *87*

9 A Snapshot of the Daily Life of the Children's Panel: Fife Child Care Inquiry *97*

10 The Scottish Children's Panel And Europe *107*

Glossary: Terms Used in the Children's Panel System *115*

Bibliography: Children's Panel System and Related Matters *122*

Index *124*

Chapter 1

Children In Trouble In Scotland

Children In Trouble In Scotland

1.1 Children drawn to public attention

Children in trouble can attract public attention by what they do or fail to do or by what adults do or fail to do to them. How is society to deal with children in trouble? For a quarter of a century the children's panel system in Scotland was thought to provide some of the answers in its unique welfare justice system as expressed and practised in a philosophy of care. The Scottish way of dealing with troubled children as expressed through the children's panel system is unique.

The children's panel is concerned with children, who are in trouble. They are the concern of any society. Children can be in trouble for what they do or fail to do. Children may come into conflict with the law because they commit offences. It is not necessarily that they misbehave in a trivial and childish manner, but many of them are involved in quite serious and disturbing crimes. Children may run away from home and be said to be beyond the control of their parents. Some children may be involved in drug misuse. Other children truant from school. In this way children attract public attention.

Children can be in trouble quite innocently and tragically. Children may be in serious trouble for what adults do to them. The German word *Kindesmisshandlung* is suggestive of child mishandling. The idea of child mishandling expresses the problem better than the English words 'child abuse'. The mishandling of children leads to the mistreatment of them often by the very people responsible for their proper upbringing and protection, namely their parents. The mishandling or maltreatment of children is an affront to any society. This mishandling of children would also include a much wider definition than suggested by child abuse, so as to include concerns about parents, who neglect or cannot give to their children proper care, causing them unnecessary suffering or resulting in their development being hampered.

In Scotland in contrast to England and Wales, in a very pragmatic way the double challenge of trouble for children arising from actions or failures, either of the children themselves or of adults, principally their parents, should be dealt with within the children's panel system in a caring manner by the practice of a care philosophy, unfortunately somewhat diluted by legislation passed by parliament in 1995.[1]

It is to be hoped that the tradition and practice of the philosophy of care in Scotland within the children's panel system from 1971 to 1996 will prove too strong to allow that philosophy to be any further weakened. The purpose of this book is to argue for the need to maintain that philosophy in the context of a radical reform of the children's panel system in order to meet the challenges of the future in promoting the welfare of children in trouble in a realistic and acceptable way. This book advocates a welfare justice system for children citing the Scottish experience as an example worthy of examination, but in need of reform.

The characteristic of welfare justice for children in trouble is a philosophy of care. Without it welfare does not exist. Welfare is about caring for children in trouble. It is about how children attracted to public attention are treated. The children's panel system must remain committed to a welfare justice approach. The commitment should be such that the children's panel and its philosophy of care are inseparable.

1.2 Children's panel principles in a philosophy of care

Care should be the starting point of what the children's panel system is about and how it should work. Prior to the Children (Scotland) Act 1995 no children's hearing decision could possibly be justified unless it was in the best interests of the child, in other words their 'paramount consideration' of 'the welfare of the child throughout his childhood'. In 1995 the law permitted a decision concerning a child to be justified on a lesser basis than the welfare of the child, where the child posed a threat of 'serious harm' to others. Without exception the child's welfare must be paramount. The child has to be cared for.

A simple way of thinking of how the child care philosophy should work within the children's panel system is to take the word 'care'. Each letter of the word points to features of the system as to how it should operate to help children.

The first letter of the word 'care', the letter 'C' could point to the word 'community'. Scots Law through the 1995 Act insists that the local community take responsibility for troubled children in their midst. Any community is principally made up of ordinary decent citizens. The children's panel in each local authority council area is composed of ordinary citizens not elected but appointed in recognition of their concern, knowledge and interest in children. In a sense the

14

members of the children's panel, called panel members, are thought of as representing their community, not in a political sense, but because they are chosen from as wide a cross section of society as possible and maintaining a close relationship with the community.[2] Perhaps the lay magistrate in England and Wales might be said to have a similar role.

In considering the problems of a child from their local community three panel members sit on a children's hearing. The spirit of care should and must direct their deliberations to do what is in the best interests of the child to promote his or her welfare.

The second letter of the word 'care', the letter 'A' highlights the word 'assessment'. In order to decide what is best for the child in terms of care the three lay panel members require professional advice. The social worker assigned to the child's case would certainly give advice. If the child is of school age a report from the school would be available. Dependent on the circumstances presented to the children's hearing other professional advice may be available, for example, from a psychologist or a psychiatrist.

The letter 'R' from the word 'care' could be said to remind panel members at a children's hearing of the rights of children and parents. For panel members this denotes a cautionary note. In a sincere desire, even with the best of motives to help children, there is always a danger that children's rights might be overlooked. It is essential that children's rights be respected. Due to the dependence of childhood, children are much more vulnerable than an adults and therefore require greater protection of their rights. The hearing has a duty to inform the family of their rights.[3]

Children's rights have to be considered in a much wider context than formal legal rights within the procedures of the children's panel system. In considering caring for children in trouble for whatever reason, their welfare and rights become intertwined. The U.N.Convention on the Rights of the Child (1989) and the earlier European Convention on Human Rights (1987) will be the standard against which in practice the children's panel system may be judged. A radical adjustment has to be made to the children's panel system in order to ensure that children's rights are respected in accordance with international standards.

Finally the last letter of the word 'care' the letter 'E' points to the word 'effort'. Care is meaningless unless it can be translated into practice by the effort to care for the child. Panel members have to insist that proper resources of care principally in the community are made available to assist the child. The local authority has a responsibility to implement any supervision requirement made by a children's hearing.

Whatever is insisted upon by the children's hearing as being in the best interests of the child in promoting the child's welfare has to be put into effect by the provision of proper resources.

1.3 The Scottish public and the children's panel

In a quarter of a century of the existence of the children's panel Scottish public opinion regarding it has fluctuated. The author, who served as a reporter to the children's panel during all of that period, remembers in 1971 the scepticism and the hostility of criticism from the public towards the then newly established children's panel system. As the years passed by children's hearings gained public confidence and credibility, not by trumpeting their own virtues, but by the experience of families in the way in which they were treated at hearings and the successful outcomes for many children in the manner in which they were assisted.

In August 1993 the Secretary of State for Scotland placed on record his confidence in 'Scotland's unique system of children's hearings' in its continuing to have 'a key role combining legal requirements, professional skills and common sense judgements of trained members of the community'.[4] This kind of confidence expressed in the children's panel system related to a consensus of belief in Scotland at that time in its underlying philosophy of care for children in trouble. The achievements of the children's panel were said to be recognised both in Scotland and elsewhere.[5]

The history of the children's panel cannot be told without reference to the Orkney and Fife Inquiries. The Orkney Inquiry report[6] into the handling of child sexual abuse allegations and the Fife Inquiry report[7] regarding child care policies were both presented to parliament on the same day on 27 October 1992. In 1993 the Court of Session ordered the retrial of child sexual abuse allegations in South Ayrshire.[8] The verdict announced in February 1995 was to overturn what had previously been found to be proved. The experiences of Orkney, Fife and South Ayrshire in some measure dented the credibility of the children's panel system.

The Children (Scotland) Act 1995 attempted to address issues raised in the Orkney, Fife and South Ayrshire particularly with regard to the rights of children. In so doing some of its enactments could be judged to be ill-conceived, resulting in weakening to some degree the philosophy and practice of care within the working of the children's panel system. After the experiences of Orkney, Fife and South Ayrshire undoubtedly reform was necessary. This book advocates a more

16

radical reform not only to recover what has been lost in the philosophy and practice of care but to address for the future the demand for a commitment to respect children's rights in Scotland in conformity to international standards.

Other European approaches to the problems of children in trouble have a great deal to teach those involved in the Scottish children's panel system. Hopefully the reverse will also be true. Scotland is part of the European Union. There will be inevitably a great deal of movement of families across national frontiers. Indeed, if truth be told, across Europe there is a tradition of a common care philosophy, albeit manifesting itself in differing systems.

ENDNOTES

1. Social Work (Scotland) Act 1968, sections 32(1), 39(3), 43(1) (repealed) and 44(1) and Children (Scotland) Act 1995, sections 16(1)(5), 39, 52(1), 56(6), 70 and 71.

2. Scottish Office: *The Structure of Local Government: Shaping the Future: The New Councils* (CM 2267), Edinburgh, HMSO 1993, paras. 3.10 and 3.11 and Local Government Etc. (Scotland) Act 1994, Part III.

3. Children's Hearings (Scotland) Rules 1986, Rule 19(4).

4. Scottish Office: *Scotland's Children: Proposals for Child Care Policy and Law* (CM 2286), Edinburgh, HMSO 1993, Foreward.

5. Finlayson, Alan F., *Reporters to Children's Panels: Their Role, Function and Accountability*, Scottish Office 1992, paras. 1.1 and 1.2. Scottish Office: *Review of Child Care Law in Scotland*, Edinburgh, HMSO 1990, para. 1.7.

6. *The Report of the Inquiry into the Removal of Children from Orkney in February 1991*, Edinburgh, HMSO 1992. (Orkney Inquiry Report)

7. *The Report of the Inquiry into Child Care Policies in Fife*, Edinburgh, HMSO 1992. (Fife Inquiry Report)

8. *L,Petitioners (No.1)* (First Div.) 1993 SLT 1310. *L, Petitioners (No.2)* (First Div.) 1993 SLT 1342.

Chapter 2

Community Responsibility for Children In Trouble

CHAPTER 2

Community Responsibility for Children In Trouble

2.1 Children's panel system unique to Scotland

Scotland has its own legal system and in some circumstances laws different from other parts of the United Kingdom. The Union Treaty of 1707 allowed Scotland to maintain its own legal tradition, although much of that has been eroded in the course of 289 years by U.K. parliamentary legislation. The reader might be tempted to think that perhaps the differences between the Scottish and English legal systems in respect of the way in which children in trouble are dealt with may quite well pre-date 1707. In fact the unique way in Scotland of coping with children's troubles by means of the children's panel system dates only from April 1971, the date of the implementation of Part III of the Social Work (Scotland) Act 1968, which is replaced by the Children (Scotland) Act 1995.

The 1968 Act brought into legislation many of the recommendations and the implied philosophy of care as outlined in a government working party report 'Children and Young Persons Scotland' published in 1964. This government working party or committee was chaired by Lord Kilbrandon, a senior Scottish judge. The remit of the working party was in essence to consider the functioning of Scottish juvenile courts in dealing with children in trouble for a variety of reasons, including delinquency, care and protection needs and being beyond parental control. The report became known as the 'Kilbrandon Report'.[1]

The conclusions of the committee in 1964 in reporting to government were in essence a break with the past. Their radical proposals called for a change in the law of Scotland in dealing with troubled children. Instead of juvenile courts the Kilbrandon committee outlined what we now know as the children's panel system. It was not so much the system outlined that was important but an underlying radical approach to the troubles of children in a philosophy of care.

2.2 The Kilbrandon Report - embryo of the Scottish children's panel system

In tackling its remit, the Kilbrandon Committee met for only 29 days. The committee, as judged by their report, approached the problems of troubled children in a practical and common sense way. The impression is justified of the committee never intending to expound a philosophy. However in their approach to problems of troubled children in terms of their proposal for a new system, a care philosophy was built up.

Early in their deliberations they concluded that there was a common background of need of care and protection regardless of the problems drawn to public attention, which children found themselves in. Traditionally care and protection seems appropriate to children suffering child abuse or lack of parental care. Perhaps the concept could be extended to other non-criminal problems of children to include assisting children, who truanted from school and refractory children beyond parental control. The genius of the committee was to determine that a further group of children, the offenders or delinquents, needed care and protection in order to tackle their problems at a much deeper level than the traditional concept of punishment could hope ever to achieve. Thus all children in trouble attracting public attention had a common need for 'special measures of education and training'. Their problems derived from their circumstances and history.

In order for the community to assist children in trouble needing special measures of education and training, the Kilbrandon Report envisaged the setting up of juvenile panels, later called children's hearings. In practical terms initially reports of all children drawn to public attention by their troubles should be sent to an official called 'the reporter'. In turn the children's reporter would refer children requiring compulsory care to the juvenile panel.

Of interest the Kilbrandon Report suggested, that whenever practical at a sitting of a juvenile panel comprising of three panel members, there should be a female panel member. Legislation eventually insisted that at a children's hearing, consisting of three panel members, there should be at least one male and one female member included.[2] The juvenile panel was to be considered as a 'locally based treatment authority'. Such a concept remained unaltered in legislation.

The juvenile panel described as 'a treatment authority' emphasises in the word 'treatment' a suggestion of a cure. The analogy is that

22

children's problems should be dealt with in a caring way as a doctor or a nurse might treat a patient. It is a useful analogy. The treatment offered to the troubled child by the juvenile panel was to be 'social education', perhaps another way of saying 'special measures of education and training'. It would be for the juvenile panel to identify the child's need for such education. The social education for the child would include principally 'social and family case work', perhaps through one to one social work counselling.

The Kilbrandon Report in it's common sense and practical approach recognised the influence of family life on a child. Social education would have to capitalise on that influence. The social worker would identify and use the positive values and influences of family life in order to help to make the treatment of the child effective. The report was at pains to emphasise 'the natural influences for good' which principally are to be found within family life. In harnessing 'those natural influences for good', the importance of enlisting the co-operation of parents was stressed. Parents could not be forced to co-operate. Perhaps the panel members at the juvenile panel would be able to persuade parents to help the child to benefit from the social education being offered.

The antithesis of care is punishment. In surveying the operation of the Scottish juvenile courts in 1964 the Kilbrandon Report rejected the old fashioned idea of dealing with offending children in terms of 'crime - responsibility - punishment'. According to the report this idea was quite inadequate to deal with the problems of children on the basis that the punishment fitting the crime might afford less to the child than care through social education to satisfy the real needs of the child in order to resolve the child's problems at a much deeper and more fundamental level. 'The needs of the individual child' would be 'the test for action' as far as the juvenile panel was to be concerned.

Difficulty might be encountered if at least the reason for concern, the allegations concerning the child, drawn to the attention of the juvenile panel, was disputed. How would a lay group of three panel members deal with issues of whether the allegation of, for example, committing an offence or having an offence committed against the child was disputed? The Kilbrandon Report wanted the panel members of the juvenile panel to concentrate on what was best for the child in terms of care in determining social education and not be distracted by disputes as to facts. Their solution was simple and clever.

Disputed allegations would be dealt with not by the juvenile panel but by the sheriff court, which in the person of the sheriff, the local judge, would have the expertise to deal with such matters. Thus faced with a dispute as to the allegations, the juvenile panel would send the case to the sheriff court for proof. If the sheriff decided that the allegations were proved, the case would return to the juvenile panel. On the basis of the allegations as accepted or proved and any other information contained in reports the juvenile panel would decide whether or not the child required compulsory care in terms of social education.

2.3 Children's panel system in action: referral of children in trouble to children's reporters

To understand how the children's panel system works in applying a care philosophy, the reader must have some understanding of its processes. The Kilbrandon Report's vision of how the juvenile panel would work was in principle translated into legislation in the Social Work (Scotland) Act 1968. There were some changes in vocabulary, notably 'the juvenile panel' became known as the 'children's hearing'. However the word 'panel' is preserved in the title of 'children's panel' consisting of the panel members of a local authority area entitled to sit on children's hearings. The title of 'reporter' survived the Kilbrandon Report.

Building on the vision of the Kilbrandon Report children, in trouble for what they themselves do or fail to do, and children, in trouble for what adults do or fail to do for them, are all treated as needing care in terms of supervision perhaps on a compulsory basis.

For whatever reason children in trouble drawn to public attention can be referred to the children's reporter by anyone considering the child requires compulsory measures of supervision. Examples include the police referring a child over eight years to the children's reporter for committing an offence; the child protection unit (a joint social work/police unit) referring a child abuse victim; a health visitor referring a child seriously lacking parental care; a teacher referring a child for truanting from school; a youth worker referring a child for solvent, drug or alcohol misuse; a social worker referring a child in moral danger and parents referring their own child for being beyond their control.

The Scottish insistence on merging of the considerations of all kinds of trouble affecting children from children in need of care and protection to children committing offences on the basis of the child's needs, differs from the English approach. The Children Act 1989 and the Criminal Justice Act 1991 in effect separated care and protection issues under civil procedure from offence cases under criminal procedure. Family proceedings courts would hear civil cases whilst youth courts dealt with child offenders.

In the Scottish children's panel system the reasons for children being in trouble are referred to in the legal jargon as 'grounds'. It is reminiscent of the German word *Grund*, meaning ground or reason. Ground denotes the foundation to build a case on, whilst reason particularises the category of the child's case. The legal jargon word 'grounds' will be used throughout the book to demonstrate both concepts.[3]

In December 1991 there were 110 children's reporters operating throughout Scotland.[4] By April 1996 children's reporters were organised into a national service following reorganisation of local authorities into 32 councils.[5]

A national service for reporters, known as the Scottish Children's Reporter Administration (S.C.R.A), headed by the principal reporter, was established with effect from April 1996, rather than their remaining in the employment of local authority councils. The Kilbrandon concept of the community emphasis of care within the children's panel system will be that bit more difficult to maintain. However the intention is that within S.C.R.A children's reporters will still maintain close links with their local communities.

The Kilbrandon Report envisaged the children's reporter's role as 'having similarities to those of a public prosecutor'. A description of the children's reporter as a public prosecutor would be inaccurate as a children's hearing is not envisaged as a court of law. Yet the children's reporter's duties in some respects have a remarkable similarity to that of a public prosecutor. Perhaps using the analogy of a para-medic, the children's reporter could be described as a para-prosecutor.

The children's reporter's role as a para-prosecutor is seen in his or her duty to assess the evidence of an allegation in respect of a child in trouble. The children's reporter as para-prosecutor has to decide whether or not the evidence is sufficient to justify the allegations or grounds to a criminal standard of beyond all reasonable doubt if the child is said to have committed an offence and to a civil standard of the balance of probabilities in all other types of grounds.[6] If the evidence is insufficient for the grounds, the children's reporter takes no further action. If there was sufficient evidence to support grounds, the children's reporter would normally take action starting with investigating the child's case further, including requesting background reports.

In taking action the children's reporter considers not only the allegations or grounds but background reports by child care professionals such as the social worker, head or guidance teacher, psychologist and psychiatrist. The children's reporter has to decide whether or not the child in his or her opinion requires compulsory measures of supervision. At this stage the children's reporter has two choices. The first choice is to divert the case away from the children's hearing if the children's reporter decides the child does not require compulsory supervision. The alternative choice is to refer the child to a children's hearing if the children's reporter believes the child requires compulsory supervision.

By diverting the case away from a children's hearing, when the children's reporter feels that a child does not require compulsory supervision the children's reporter has a number of options. The children's reporter might simply decide not to do anything, so that the decision would be formally no further action. If the child is a first time offender, committing a relatively trivial offence, the children's reporter might be persuaded to refer the case back to the police to warn the child. Care is related to the children's reporter contacting the social worker to arrange voluntary social work support or supervision for the child with the agreement of the family.

2.4 Children's panel system in action: referral of children in trouble to children's hearings

The children's reporter may decide that the child does require compulsory supervision. In such circumstances the children's reporter refers the child to the children's hearing and prepares a statement referred to often as the grounds of referral. By formulating and signing his or her statement of grounds, the children's reporter affirms his or her belief in good faith that there is sufficient evidence, that is, that in his or her opinion the grounds are 'established'.

Most children who appear before children's hearings along with their parents accept the children's reporter's statement of grounds. The children are able to understand the hearing chairman's explanation of the grounds. Once the grounds are accepted the hearing is able to proceed further with the case.

The Kilbrandon Report's solution to disputed grounds has been incorporated into legislation, that is, that the sheriff will decide on the truth or otherwise of the facts and the children's hearing with whether or not the child requires compulsory supervision. Thus when the family appear before the hearing and deny the grounds, the three panel members have a choice either to discharge the grounds or send the case for proof to the sheriff.

Assuming the grounds are considered by the sheriff in a proof hearing, which resembles a trial held in private, the children's reporter acts as prosecutor, whilst the family is represented by a solicitor. If the sheriff finds the grounds proved or established in whole or in part, the sheriff sends the case back to the hearing for the hearing to decide the issue of compulsory care for the child. The sheriff will discharge the grounds if the grounds are not proved.

A similar procedure occurs where the child is unable to understand an explanation of the grounds due to intellect or age.

Prior to considering the child's case at the children's hearing the three panel members will have studied not only the children's reporter's statement of grounds but also background reports from the social worker, school, or any other professional involved in the child's case.

Sometimes on a few occasions the panel members feel they do not have enough information to reach a decision. The case may have to be continued for further reports to a later children's hearing. In the meanwhile the child may require to be kept in a place of safety for a period of up to 22 days. To do so the hearing would issue a warrant which can be renewed on application by the children's reporter. It is possible for a child to be held in a place of safety under warrants on the authority of a hearing for up to 66 days. Prior to the expiry of a hearing warrant the sheriff on application of the children's reporter could grant a warrant to keep the child in a place of safety specifying the duration of the warrant. A child could at least in theory be kept temporarily in a place of safety for a period beyond 66 days without limit to the sheriff's discretion as to the duration of the warrant or the number of occasions of its renewal.[7]

Continued cases are the exception rather than the rule. The children's hearing is more likely to be able to move on from the acceptance of the grounds by the family, or the grounds having been found proved by the sheriff, to consider reports and reach a decision. If the hearing does not think compulsory supervision is necessary, the hearing would discharge the grounds. Otherwise if compulsory supervision is necessary in the hearing's view, the child would be placed on a supervision requirement.

A supervision requirement could require the child to be supervised by a social worker whilst the child remains at home, or requires the child to reside with a foster parent (carer), or insists the child be received into residential care to stay in a children's home or residential school, inclusive of, in exceptional cases, the child being liable to be placed in secure accommodation. The supervision lasts for a maximum of a year but must be reviewed by the hearing before the end of the year. A review may be requested at any time by the social worker concerned with the child's case, or after three months by the child or parent. If a child appearing before a children's hearing is on a supervision requirement, the hearing is required to review that supervision requirement as part of it's consideration of the child's case. The hearing may include a date for the review as a condition in a supervision requirement. At a review hearing the decisions open to the hearing are to continue, vary or terminate the supervision requirement.

The procedure at a children's hearing could be described as informal. The three panel members try to make the family feel at ease so as to facilitate dialogue. Every effort is made to encourage the child to speak. The hearing is particularly anxious to listen to what the child has to say. There are of course rules governing the conduct of the hearing but they are not unduly restrictive. The intention is to create hopefully a dialogue between the hearing and the family in order to reach a sensible solution to the child's problems.

In practice the children's hearing is a forum for discussion. The three panel members in meeting the parents and child discuss the difficulties which the child or family may be facing and together try to seek solutions. The discussion in large measure is informed by reports presented by child care professionals. These reports are sent out in advance of the hearing's date to the three panel members for their study and preparation. At the hearing the family are informed of the substance of the reports by the chairman.

If the child or parents at a children's hearing are feeling somewhat apprehensive or tense, it must be difficult for them to fully comprehend what is being said about them in reports, despite the best efforts of the chairman and his or her colleagues. If parents were provided with copies of reports in advance of the hearing, it would greatly assist the discussion at the hearing. The chairman could still helpfully highlight briefly the issues of concern contained in reports. The parents and even the child, depending on his or her maturity, would be much better prepared to participate in dialogue.

Appeal can be made to the sheriff against a children's hearing decision, either against the hearing issuing a warrant to keep the child in a place of safety for no more than 22 days, or against a supervision requirement. The children's reporter is present at the appeal to put forward the case on behalf of the hearing's decision. The family is represented by a solicitor, who would argue against the hearing's decision.

In considering the decision of the children's hearing the sheriff may hear evidence from or on behalf of the family. If the appeal is against a warrant for the child to be kept temporarily in a place of safety, the sheriff either confirms or recalls the warrant. If a supervision requirement has been made by the hearing, the sheriff can confirm the hearing's decision, order that a condition making the child liable to be placed in secure accommodation shall cease to have effect, substitute his or her own decision by imposing a supervision requirement different from that imposed by the hearing, send the case back to the hearing for their re-consideration, or discharge the case entirely.

There is an appeal open to the family or the children's reporter against the sheriff's decision to the sheriff principal or the Court of Session, the highest civil court in Scotland, and against the sheriff principal's decision to the Court of Session on a point of law.

The additional powers given to the sheriff by the Children (Scotland) Act 1995 on an appeal in effect to re-hear the case in listening to evidence presented by or on behalf of the family, and the right of the sheriff to substitute his or her own decision for that of the children's hearing by imposing a supervision requirement different from that imposed by the hearing, weakens the standing of hearings. Rather than hearings being weakened they require to be strengthened perhaps by introducing the concept of a children's judge sitting with two panel members and upgrading the status of the hearing to that of a children's court.

ENDNOTES

1. *Children and Young Persons Scotland* (1964), Edinburgh HMSO 1995, paras. 3, 13, 17, 35, 39, 54(1), 73, 77(title), 92, 98-102, 108, and 138. (The Kilbrandon Report).

2. Children (Scotland) Act 1995, sections 39, 51, 52, 56, 65, 66, 68-70 and 73.

3. Children's Hearing (Scotland) Rules 1986, Rules 6, 16, 19 and 21.

4. Finlayson, Alan F., *Reporters to Children's Panels: Their Role, Function and Accountability*, Scottish Office 1992, para. 2.6.

5. Scottish Office: *The Structure of Local Government: Shaping the Future:The New Councils* (CM 2267), Edinburgh, HMSO 1993, paras. 1.3 and 3.11 and Local Government Etc. (Scotland) Act 1994, Part III.

6. *Harris v F.* [1991], SLT 242F.

7. Norrie, Kenneth McK., *Children (Scotland) Act 1995* (Greens Annotated Acts), W. Green/Sweet and Maxwell 1995 pages 36/67.

Chapter 3

Community In Action Through The Children's Panel

CHAPTER 3

Community In Action Through The Children's Panel

3.1 Children's Panel Advisory Committee

The role of the panel member is crucial to the success of the children's panel system in Scotland. At any one time there are about 1,750 panel members sitting on children's hearings in Scotland.[1] It is the three panel members forming a children's hearing, who take the decision as to whether or not a child in trouble is to be placed on a supervision requirement, insisting that the child requires compulsory supervision. It is only their decisions, and not the children's reporters', which are appealable to the sheriff.

If children's hearings are to have any credibility with the Scottish public, there must be respect for panel members. It is therefore essential that a panel member is of good calibre and respected by the community. The question as to how they are appointed in the first place is of prime importance.

The Kilbrandon Report of 1964 envisaged that the sheriff would appoint panel members in a particular area and decide who amongst them would be the chairman and two deputy chairmen for each children's panel.[2] However this was not to be. By 1968 the decision had been made, enshrined in legislation, that a children's panel advisory committee (C.P.A.C.) for each local authority area should select suitable persons to be panel members. The C.P.A.C. would recommend such persons so selected to the Secretary of State for Scotland for appointment. It would be the Secretary of State's decision as to who were actually appointed. The Secretary of State would initially appoint panel members for say a three year period of office. That appointment could be and often was renewed on recommendation by the C.P.A.C. The appointment by the Secretary of State was considered as perhaps giving a status to panel members.

The composition of the C.P.A.C. emphasises the community orientation of the children's panel system. The C.P.A.C. itself is made up of three appointees appointed by the Secretary of State, usually local people and often former panel members, and two members

33

usually councillors from the social work committee appointed by the local authority council. The membership of the C.P.A.C. can be increased by the Secretary of State for Scotland on the application of the local authority of up to five additional members. The chairman of the C.P.A.C. is always drawn from one of the government appointees. The idea is that C.P.A.C. members with local knowledge of their communities would be able to recommend suitable people with a concern for children as possible panel members.

The community orientation is further emphasised in the efforts of the C.P.A.C. to ensure that those recommended to be panel members are drawn from as wide a cross section of the community as possible. Each year advertisements in local and national newspapers as well as on television appear asking ordinary people to apply to be panel members.

Once a panel member is regularly serving on children's hearings, the C.P.A.C. has a further responsibility to monitor the panel member's performance at hearings. Is the panel member sensibly, appropriately and sensitively considering children's cases at hearings? The C.P.A.C. member assigned to attend the hearing to observe a particular panel member would wish to be assured that the panel member was living up to the C.P.A.C.'s expectations of that member, when the C.P.A.C. initially selected and recommended the panel member for appointment. Assuming the C.P.A.C. member observing at the hearing was satisfied that this was so, there would be the possibility of a recommendation towards the end of the period of appointment for re-appointment of the panel member by the Secretary of State for a further period of office. Some panel members have served for 12 or more years.

There may be occasions when the C.P.A.C. member is not satisfied with regard to the panel member's performance. If the performance does not improve on further observation, the panel member may not be recommended for re-appointment. Sadly in exceptional circumstances the behaviour of a panel member may be such as to indicate his or her unsuitability to continue to be a panel member. The C.P.A.C. would so recommend to the Secretary of State, who would order that the panel member's name be removed from the list of the children's panel.

Although the C.P.A.C.'s principal function is to select suitable persons to be recommended for appointment or re-appointment as panel members by the Secretary of State, the C.P.A.C. has other obligations, which gives it considerable influence in the children's panel system. Having sought out suitable people to be panel members, the C.P.A.C. always takes an interest in their training. At meetings of the C.P.A.C. matters of general interest in the children's panel system are discussed.

3.2 Essential qualities and demands of being a panel member as representing the community

The most obvious thing to say is that the panel member, representing the community, when he or she sits to consider children's cases at a children's hearing, is an ordinary citizen. Equally obvious are the qualities and expectations as indicated in the 1964 Kilbrandon Report. The would be panel member should be a person with knowledge, experience and empathy for children. The panel member's work and attendance at children's hearings would be voluntary. Although part time, the work would demand a great deal of commitment.

In the context of volunteering to be panel members and to carry out their unpaid duties, other than reimbursement of expenses, the commitment expected of panel members is quite remarkable. They are expected to undertake both initial and in-service training. On average a panel member would be expected to attend approximately a three hour session of children's hearings twice a month, to consider on each occasion possibly 3 cases. Even attending a hearing session for three hours at a time is the least demanding of time of the panel member. For about every three quarters of an hour of the hearing to consider a case, the panel member has to spend at least double that time in preparation at home in reading and reflecting on the case papers of the child.

The panel member being an ordinary citizen is expected to apply what is called common sense. Yet this is a quality which is so ill-defined, but so essential. Perhaps it is an unseen form of wisdom. The meaning of common sense might be conveyed in the German words *gesunder Menschenverstand*, which could be literally translated as 'healthy human understanding'. The public have a great respect for what we call common sense or healthy human understanding. In exercising common sense it is hoped that a panel member will behave in a kindly, considerate and sympathetic manner.

The panel member should be free of racial, religious or gender prejudice. The C.P.A.C. would have to weed out applicants for membership of the panel who were inclined to reveal any such prejudice. The selectors would also have to exclude applicants who reveal an attitude, for example, in dealing with offending behaviour of being overtly punitive.

It has already been said that panel members spend more time preparing for a children's hearing than actually being present at one. They need to study case papers or reports prior to the hearing. The C.P.A.C. selectors are very much aware that those, who aspire to be panel members, must be able to read, understand and assimilate reports, drawing out salient points. The illiterate could not obviously be appointed as panel members. The demands of reading and understanding often volumes of reports regarding a number of cases at a particular hearing places the C.P.A.C. selectors in a quandary in their endeavours to ensure that those, who are recommended to be panel members, are drawn from as wide a cross section of society as possible.

The panel member does not work alone but has to co-operate with his or her two colleague panel members at the children's hearing. The 3 panel members are involved during the hearing in a discussion not only amongst themselves but with the family, social worker, children's reporter and if attending, other professionals. Thus the C.P.A.C. would have to be satisfied that the applicant to become a panel member would be able to take part in group discussion. During the selection process applicants are invited to take part in discussion groups and in so doing are observed and assessed. Persons who are too timid to speak, or at the other extreme too domineering, are unlikely to be selected. Successful applicants will be those observed to be comfortable in such a setting as well as showing an inclination to listen, consider views, and make constructive points.

Panel members, of course, should be of good character. It would be quite invidious at a children's hearing if a parent were able with justification to make the comment that a panel member sitting in judgement on his or her child, for example, had served a prison sentence. Any serving panel member, who has the misfortune to appear in court pleading guilty, or being convicted of an offence, would have the decency to realise that he or she had to submit his or her resignation immediately. A police check is done on applicants for panel membership to ensure that if they were appointed there would not be the embarrassment of their having previous convictions. It would be quite outrageous, if someone was appointed as a panel member who had a previous record, for example, of abusing children. On a positive note panel members should be of good standing in their communities, otherwise how could they possibly have the respect of families, who appear before hearings in their locality.

3.3 Panel member training

Emphasising that panel members are essentially ordinary people, good citizens, with a concern for children, the question immediately arises as to whether that is enough. Even with the best intentions and motives much more is needed for a panel member to consider the difficulties of children, than a panel member simply being an ordinary person. Even although there are professionals to advise them at children's hearings as to what is best to do for the children, is it really sensible that professionalism, namely the advice of professionals, should be subject to amateurism of good ordinary citizens? The doubts raised about the propriety of such amateurism would almost be unassailable if their being law abiding citizens and being concerned for children was all that was required of panel members.

For the first four or five months of their appointment the panel members do not take part in children's hearings. During this time the panel member participates in part time initial training. They learn about the children's panel system, inclusive of procedures and powers of children's hearings, the care philosophy and other related issues such as child development.

Once the panel member has completed the initial four or five months training and becomes as it were a full panel member serving on children's hearings, training is far from finished. In fact throughout the years of being a panel member, regardless of experience, the panel member is expected to attend in-service training when arranged.

The criticism of amateurism of panel members has to be properly addressed. To suggest that the part time training of panel members is sufficient to overcome that criticism is not sustainable. The criticism can only be overcome by the introduction of a professional children's judge as chairman of each hearing, upgraded to a children's court to sit perhaps with two lay panel members. The presence of the two panel members would retain the community aspect.

3.4 Children's hearings as seen by families

Panel members representing the community at children's hearings as ordinary people is not something which is confined to theory. Families who attend hearings are very much aware that those facing them in a sense across the table, are three ordinary people from their own community.

On their side of the table there would of course be the two parents, hopefully, and the child. The parent and child both have a right to be present during the whole of the children's hearing. Although the child is required to attend the hearing, the panel members can in certain circumstances excuse the child's attendance. The circumstance might relate to the child being a victim of an offence or in other circumstances where it might be detrimental to the 'safeguarding or promotion of the child's welfare' to be present.[3]

Given the parental right to be present at all stages of the children's hearing, difficulty may be experienced if parents exercised their rights in all circumstances. Occasion may arise when the three panel members sense that the child is too afraid to speak in his or her parents' presence. The Kilbrandon Report suggested that there might be a reason for the juvenile panel to talk with the child alone. The hearing can exclude the parents from the whole or part of the hearing when to do so is the only way to obtain the views of the child. If the parents' presence at the hearing 'is causing or is likely to cause significant distress to the child' the hearing can exclude them. However afterwards the chairman of the hearing must disclose to them the substance of the discussion with the child. The chairman's duty so to do might be argued as considering the exclusion of the parent as pointless.

The three panel members have to discuss the child's problems with the child and his or her parents. If the discussion is to be fruitful, the discussion should take place in an informal and comfortable setting. Walking into the hearing room the family might find a rectangular table with the three panel members sitting on one side and the family expected to sit opposite. The children's reporter and social worker might sit at either end of the table with guidance teacher or other child care professional sitting where there is a space around the table. A more informal setting of low chairs around a small coffee table, or indeed no table at all, might be preferred. Hearing rooms can vary from the luxurious to the spartan. Whatever setting is chosen for the children's hearing, a relative informality may be apparent in order to encourage maximum participation by families in discussion. The whole purpose of having a hearing room comfortable is in order to aid communication between the three panel members and the family at the hearing.

3.5 The informal agenda at a children's hearing

The c'aim has already been made that the Scottish children's panel syst₁ ,n is the local community caring for it's own troubled children. The test of how it does so is to be seen in how children's hearings actually work in a caring attitude towards children in trouble. How do the representatives of the community, namely the three panel members, consider a child's case and deliberate on the child's problems? How do the family feel about being at the hearing? How are they encouraged to talk about their problems? How is the child to be encouraged to talk about him or herself at the hearing? How are parents, who know the child best, to contribute to the discussion?

The three panel members representing the local community have to talk through the problems with the family and ascertain where solutions may lie. The child care professionals attending the hearing work locally within the community usually living in or near to the community. These professionals of course include the children's reporter for the area, the case responsible social worker, the headteacher or other teacher from the school if the child is of school age and, dependent on the circumstances of the child, a psychologist or consultant child psychiatrist. The danger is always that the family could be overawed by the whole proceedings and those who are present. The proceedings or the agenda has to be such as to allow an informality in order to encourage the family to participate in the hearing as intended.

Regardless of how distressing the grounds or allegations may be, it is important that the family are welcomed by the chairman of the children's hearing, one of the three panel members. The three panel members, inclusive of the panel member chosen to be chairman, are usually selected for a particular hearing session by the chairman of the children's panel.[4] The introductions and welcoming of the family by the chairman is the first attempt to break down barriers. The family are perhaps feeling tense, uncomfortable and embarrassed. Such feelings have to be overcome if dialogue is to take place between the three representatives of the community and the family.

The chairman is obliged to tell the family the purpose of the hearing. If the purpose is to consider grounds the chairman explains what is stated in the children's reporter's statement of grounds to ascertain whether or not they are accepted by the family.

Assuming that the grounds are accepted by the family, a short discussion on the grounds will follow. Being local, the panel members may, for example, know the exact place where an offence by a child occurred, making it easier for them to understand how and why the child committed the offence. If the child truanted from school, the headteacher or teacher present will be able to shed some light on perhaps why the child fails to attend school properly. In care and protection cases, such as abuse, neglect or lack of parental care, the panel members may have some sympathy regarding the predicament in which the parents find themselves perhaps, for example, in their living in poor housing or suffering the distress of unemployment.

It could be quite off-putting for a family to be faced across the table with the three panel members looking at reports about them from the social worker, headteacher and other child care professionals. Great care is taken by the chairman to describe and explain to them what is said in the reports, giving them a chance to respond. The grounds are considered in the context of the child's own background, so that a proper and not a distorted understanding is gained about the child. This sets the agenda for the hearing.

The major part of the children's hearing is taken up in discussion. The most important participant in that discussion at the hearing is the child. In fact the hearing is required by law to obtain the views of the child taking into account the child's maturity. A child of at least the age of 12 years is assumed to be able to form a view. In other words the hearing should endeavour to elicit what the child feels and thinks.

Any observer at a children's hearing would testify as to the efforts made by panel members to encourage children to speak to them. Time will be spent trying to get the child to say even a few words. Success and failure in this regard abound. Some children, when encouraged, are quite talkative, whilst others perhaps with eyes cast down to the floor refuse to say even one word. The panel members cannot be faulted for at least trying.

Children at children's hearings tend to talk more when they are happy and not depressed. They are more inclined to speak when they are praised rather than when they feel under threat of being criticised. It is very difficult for a child to talk perhaps when he or she feels ashamed or embarrassed at having committed an offence. Children find it difficult to describe how or explain why they committed offences. At other times children will speak with very little inhibition, telling the panel members about what has been happening to them at home or school.

Panel members feel that the children's hearing is much more rewarding if children are persuaded to fully participate. The words 'children's hearing' are simply an indication that panel members and others at the hearing have a duty to hear what the child says.

The aim of the discussion is try to reach a consensus between the panel members, the family and the child care professionals present. As a result of the consensus the family might agree to voluntary arrangements so that compulsory supervision is unnecessary. Although it may sound illogical, a decision for compulsory supervision may be the result of a consensus. The worried mother or father concerned about their delinquent son might feel after discussion at the hearing that compulsory supervision is their only hope to stop their son offending. Unaided they themselves cannot do so. The child may not listen to them but may listen to the social worker.

Panel members' decisions at children's hearings are usually reached unanimously. This of course would be the case if the three panel members had reached a consensus with the family. However it has to be admitted that there are occasions where panel members may reach a decision concerning which the family object. There are also occasions where the decision is made on a majority of two panel members to one. A majority decision hearing is by no means a failure. Looked at positively, the family may have the feeling that the decision has not been arrived at prior to the hearing, which of course should never happen.

The decision is made in the presence of the family and reasons given. The family is informed of their rights, inclusive of their right to appeal against the decision if the hearing has insisted on compulsory care. This part of the hearing should not be underestimated. Regard for children's rights is essential for a proper respect for the child.

ENDNOTES

1. Scottish Office: *Twenty One Years of Children's Hearings*, 1992, page 7.

2. Lockyear, Andrew and Wilkinson, David, *Citizens Serving Children*, Scottish Office 1992, pages 15-17 and *Children and Young Persons Scotland* (1964), Edinburgh HMSO 1995, paras. 92 and 108. (The Kilbrandon Report).

3. Children (Scotland) Act 1995, sections 6(1), 16(2), 39(2) 45, 46, 51, 65 and 70 and Schedule 1.

4. Children's Hearings (Scotland) Rules 1986, rules 5(1) and 19(1)-(4).

Chapter 4

Lay and Professional in the Children's Panel System

Lay and Professional in the Children's Panel System

4.1 Children's hearing as a lay tribunal and alternatives

The emphasis so far regarding the Scottish children's panel system is that the children's panel is the expression of the community taking responsibility for troubled children within its midst. The vehicle for that responsibility is the children's hearing. The three panel members at the hearing are ordinary people from the community albeit with an interest and concern for children and having undergone part-time training.

How therefore can the children's hearing of three ordinary citizen panel members be best described? Perhaps one way of doing so is to state what it is not. Although dealing with, for example, delinquent children, the hearing is not a court of law. Despite the claim that the three panel members sitting as a hearing is the community in action dealing with its own problem children, the hearing is not a committee of the local authority council. It essentially remains what it is, namely, a meeting of three good citizens appointed as panel members, because they are concerned for children in trouble and are anxious to resolve their problems.

The children's hearing is a lay tribunal. Any hearing sitting can be visited by a member of the Council on Tribunals or its Scottish committee for the purpose of monitoring its procedures as a tribunal.[1] The status of tribunal indicates that the hearing, although not a court of law, is a judicial body taking decisions regarding children with the authority of law.

An argument in favour of the lay tribunal is that professional advice, as conveyed through reports to and discussions at the children's hearing, is tested as to whether it is acceptable to the community. Panel members being drawn from the community should be able to sense what is acceptable or otherwise to that community. Their decision at the end of the hearing should be a reflection of the community's reaction to the problems of the child, tempered by the best professional advice available. Compulsory supervision should not be imposed on a child without public scrutiny and acceptance.

Any doubts about the possible defect of a lay children's hearing tribunal could be said to be dispelled when consideration is given to the acceptance or otherwise of hearings' decisions by families. The scarcity of appeals against hearings' decisions may prove the case in favour of the lay hearing.[2] Families appearing before hearings in the vast majority of cases are prepared to accept their decisions. Perhaps they feel that their decisions often equate with common sense. Families are in some respects a party to these decisions in the dialogues, which take place at hearings. They are prepared to accept the decisions as fair.

The majority of appeals by families against decisions of children's hearings fail, meaning that the sheriffs agreed with the hearings' decisions. In 1994 in Scotland of 160 such appeals to sheriffs 79 per cent (126) failed with the hearings' decisions being confirmed.[3]

The proposition that panel members should be elected locally or be elected councillors of the local authority council is difficult to counter, if panel members are claiming to represent the community. If the elected principle were to be favoured the easiest way to give expression to such a principle would be for the children's panel to be a local authority committee. The holding of a children's hearing would be a meeting of a sub-committee of three councillors.

The disadvantage might be that elected panel members or councillors might become subject to undue local pressure in particular cases or issues in the knowledge that they would have to face a future election contest. Children's hearings must take their decisions without fear or favour.

Within the functioning of the children's panel system, a concession has been made to the representation of the community being elective as far as panel members are concerned in the composition of the Children's Panel Advisory Committee (C.P.A.C) containing five members two of whom are councillors, who as C.P.A.C members have their role to play in the selection of panel members for recommendation for appointment or reappointment and in the monitoring of their performance.

The suggestion could be made that the three panel members should be professionally trained in perhaps one of a number of relevant disciplines such as social work, education, psychology, psychiatry or child care law. It is certainly an attractive suggestion. The panel members so qualified might be better able to judge the professional advice of their peers. The disadvantage might simply be that as compared to lay panel members, they could be said not to have the common touch. Lay panel members have a remarkable facility to gain the confidence of families coming before children's hearings.

Further the professionals might be at risk of becoming tied up with their own professionalism, unable to have a wider perspective.

An attractive compromise between the lay and the professional panel member might be a mixture of both in order to gain the best of both worlds. The chairman of a children's hearing could be required to be a solicitor specialising in child care law sitting with two lay panel members. The hearing so constituted would have the benefit of a full or part-time legal chairman giving an authority and professionalism to the proceedings, whilst the lay panel members would be able to retain what has already been claimed for them in representing the community, their 'common touch'.

At the other extreme from the three lay panel members of the children's hearing, the possibility of replacing the three lay panel members by a children's judge has an attraction. The children's judge could have qualifications and experience both in law and social work. Alternatively a qualification could be added to the law degree giving a particular specialism in child care law and social work, tailored to meet the requirements of the post of a children's judge. Being full time on the job the children's judge would rapidly build up experience and become accepted within the community.

The children's judge would be a professional and as such have the attributes, which could not be rivalled by the amateurism of the three lay panel members. The consequence might be argued that there would be an improved standard of judgement. Perhaps it might even encourage a better presentation of advice from professionals, whose advice would be subject to professional scrutiny.

The argument against having a children's judge would be that to have such a judge would take away from the children's panel system the sense of the community actually taking responsibility for troubled children in their midst. During 25 years panel members, serving on children's hearings, have served children well in their consideration of cases.

Perhaps the question could be reasonably asked as to why the Scottish children's panel system should not consider having, as it were, the best of both worlds. The children's judge would give to the children's hearing a better prestige. The hearing would have a heightened status of a children's court rather than merely a tribunal. The community could still be represented by two panel members, who would sit with the children's judge acting as chairman of the hearing or court. The two panel members would not only retain the element of the representation of the community but a link with the achievements of the past.

47

4.2 Lay children's hearings and courts

If the Scottish children's panel system, as it is at present, is depicted as a lay dominated the assertion is untrue. Certainly the children's hearing is a lay tribunal, but it is not the whole story. The community taking responsibility for the problems of children applying good common sense was thought to be a bit too risky, particularly if totally relied on. It had to be kept in check. The power of the lay hearing could be said to be almost eclipsed by that given to the sheriff by the Children (Scotland) Act 1995.

Until the 1995 Act the children's panel system was a compromise between a system of lay children's hearings, the community in action, and the highly professional legal judge as depicted by the sheriff and the judges of the Court of Session, the highest civil court in Scotland.[4] After the implementation of the 1995 Act the sheriff principal would also be involved. This compromise was best depicted by a scale evenly balanced between the activities of the children's reporter, who is not necessarily a lawyer, and the lay children's hearing on the one side and on the other side of the scale the activities of the professional judges, the sheriffs and the judges of the Court of Session.

On the opposite arm of the scale to the court, the children's reporter in his or her decisions in diverting children away from children's hearings is not subject to the influence of the courts. To balance the scales the children's reporter in referring any child to a hearing is always potentially subject to the influence of the courts. There is the possibility in presenting a statement of grounds to the hearing that the grounds will be denied or not understood and be sent to the sheriff court for proof. The children's reporter is well aware that such a sending for proof is a test of his or her credibility. The children's reporter may also find him or herself in the sheriff court in answering an appeal against the decision of the hearing. The sheriff's decision in turn would be in a minority of cases subject to appeal to the sheriff principal or the Court of Session.

The close relationship between the children's hearing and the sheriff is further demonstrated in certain procedures following on a child in need of care and protection being taken to a place of safety. The authority for so doing would in most cases be sought from the sheriff, who may grant a child protection order if satisfied of the child suffering or likely to suffer 'significant harm' on account of a reasonable suspicion of the child being abused or neglected. The sheriff would also have to be convinced that urgent enquiry was necessary in order to decide whether or not steps had to be taken to safeguard the child's welfare and such enquiry was being frustrated by denial of

48

access to the child. Other than the children's reporter authorising the release of the child from the place of safety, the order could continue in effect beyond the second working day, after the sheriff granted the order, only if the hearing so decided and for no more than about one week.

Other than granting a child protection order, if the sheriff were satisfied of a suspicion that the child was suffering or likely to suffer significant harm, the sheriff could issue a child assessment order requiring, for example, the parent to make the child available for assessment as specified in the order, which could even include a condition of the child for a specified period residing outwith the family home in order for the assessment to be made. The order would remain in force for no more than a week. Rather than remove the child from home another recourse available to the sheriff in order to protect the child is for the sheriff to grant an exclusion order against a suspected child abuser excluding that person from the child's home. Both the children's reporter and the children's hearing would as necessary be aware of these orders in the context of a co-operative endeavour to assist children in these kinds of difficulty.

The courts, children's reporters and hearings are brought closer together in a shared concern for the welfare of children in a number of other procedures available to them. A child could be referred to the children's reporter by the court following the conviction of an adult for an offence against the child, certifying the grounds of referral to be established.[5] In proceedings relating to divorce, separation, parental responsibilities or rights and adoption, the sheriff may refer a child to the children's reporter to arrange a children's hearing for a non-offence ground, certifying the ground to be established. The local authority may request a review of a supervision requirement in circumstances of their intending to apply to the court for a parental responsibilities order or an order freeing the child or placing a child for adoption. In the consideration of the case at the review apart from their decision on the review in respect of the supervision requirement the hearing would prepare a report advising the court as to what they considered to be in the child's best interest.[6]

4.3 Cases considered by the Court of Session: case law

Only a small number of cases are considered by the Court of Session on appeal from sheriffs' or sheriffs' principal decisions. All these cases originated from the consideration of cases by children's hearings. The influence of the deliberations of the Court of Session is considerable even although such deliberations arise from a very small number of cases. This acted as a significant counterweight in terms of the influence of the court or legal professionalism in order to balance the amateurism of the lay hearing.

The decisions of the Court of Session in the build up of case law have been very positive and supportive of the lay children's hearing.

The case law arising from Court of Session decisions have promoted a realistic care philosophy. Four examples are of interest. A children's hearing in deciding on compulsory supervision is not merely confined to consideration of the grounds, but should take into consideration the wider background of the child.[6] The children's reporter's statement of grounds regarding a child being a victim of abuse does not have to identify the abuser, as it may be only possible to state that the child was abused but impossible to identify the abuser.[7] Parents in their parenting of children are not expected to reach perfection. All that is expected is for them to act responsibly for their children within what is reasonable for them to accomplish.[8] Lack of parental care likely to cause unnecessary suffering or impairment of development can be inferred from the parents' way of life, even although the parents have not had any opportunity to care for the child as in the case of a recently born baby.[9]

Within the children's panel system the balance between the lay amateurism and legal professionalism was a healthy one. The relationship between children's hearings and courts was positive. The laity of the panel members has been generally supported by the legal professionalism of the judges in a common objective of promoting the welfare of troubled children.

4.4 Suggested radical reform of the children's panel system

With the enactment of the Children (Scotland) Act 1995 the delicate balance between the lay children's hearing and the courts has been tilted in favour of the courts with the potential of almost eclipsing the role of the hearing.

The 1995 Act gives power given to the sheriff on appeal to substitute his or her own decision for that of the children's hearing. The sheriff is enabled in effect to rehear the case again. Apart from the sheriff questioning the children's reporter or any authors of reports to the hearing, the sheriff can hear evidence from or on behalf of the child, parent and the children's reporter on account of their being parties to the proceedings.[10] Thus the proceedings of the hearing could become of little effect with the sheriff court being the real venue of decision making with appeal later to the sheriff principal or the Court of Session. The sheriff would be unlikely to have any qualification or specialist knowledge of child development or welfare.

The arena of effective decision making should be returned to the children's hearing perhaps reformed as a children's court with a children's judge sitting with two panel members. The hearing should be strengthened rather than weakened. It could be further suggested in a possible rationalisation of the process that the children's judge might well take over some of the duties of the sheriff, such as sitting alone and hearing proofs following denial of grounds.

The children's hearing or court with the children's judge along with the 2 panel members would be well equipped to deal with other matters concerning children presently the responsibility of the sheriff such as the child protection order, assessment order, exclusion order, parental responsibilities order, custody, adoption and other related child welfare matters. The children's judge should have the same status as the sheriff. Appeal against the children's judge sitting alone or with 2 panel members might be to the sheriff principal or perhaps a senior children's judge and beyond the sheriff principal or senior children's judge to the Court of Session.

4.5 Children, who commit the most serious offences, the concern of the courts: issues arising for the Scottish children's panel system from the Bulger case in England in 1993

Since the inception of the children's panel system in Scotland in 1971 there has been an acceptance within the system itself that children committing very serious offences should not at least in the first instance have their cases considered by children's reporters and children's hearings. It is recognised as part of the balance within the system of the lay children's hearing and the professional legalism of the courts. The merits of having children, who commit serious offences, dealt with by adult courts might seem to be best justified in cases of murder committed by children. Fortunately the occasions of children committing murder are extremely rare.

Regardless of the rarity of instances of murder committed by children, the issue of how such children should be dealt with has to be thought through afresh. The opportunity to do so is provided in reflecting on the English experience of the Bulger murder case at

51

Preston Crown in November 1993. If a similar murder had occurred in Scotland the trial process would in essence have been much the same. The debate arising from the Bulger case in England calls into question how children, who commit serious offences, should be most appropriately dealt with.

The terrible death of two-year-old James Bulger from Merseyside on 12 February 1993 is a tragedy beyond belief. The culprits were two 10 year old boys, who had just reached the age in accordance with English law of criminal responsibility. James was abducted by the two boys within the Strand shopping centre in Bootle whilst his mother's attention was momentarily distracted. James' body with horrific injuries was later found on a nearby railway line. By the time of their trial in Preston Crown Court in November 1993, which was reported widely in the media, the two boys were 11 years old. They were found guilty of the abduction and murder of James Bulger and their identities were revealed. Their sentence was to be detained 'during her Majesty's pleasure', understood by most to be the juvenile equivalent to a life sentence. The trial judge recommended that the two boys should serve at least eight years.[11]

The issues as relevant for Scotland as England arising from the James Bulger trial are threefold, namely, (i) putting the two accused boys on trial in an adult court, (ii) the age of criminal responsibility and (iii) their sentence.

Reflecting on media publicity of what occurred during this trial, the question has to be asked: was the trial in this form for two eleven year old boys appropriate? Has the thought that a child should be treated as a child and not an adult to be abandoned even for the children, who commit the most serious crimes? The logic of an affirmative answer is untenable, suggesting that the most serious delinquents have a level of intelligence far beyond their years! Rather than the children, committing serious crimes, being tried and convicted in adult courts, perhaps the experience of the Bulger trial suggests that they could be dealt with by a special children's court.

In the Scottish context the problem might be resolved in the context of a radically reformed children's hearing upgraded to the status of a court with a children's judge sitting with two panel members. Reflecting on the gravity of the situation if the hearing or children's court was not acceptable a special children's court outwith the criminal court system could be convened with a senior judge advised by two children's judges.

The age of 11 years of the two boys on trial for murder raises the issue of the age of criminal responsibility as to whether or not it is too low at eight years in Scotland and ten years in England. However the issue would not be of particular concern provided children regardless of the seriousness of their offences were kept out of the criminal justice system. In Scotland this would be the case with a radically reformed children's hearing upgraded to a children's court or, if necessary to consider very serious offences committed by children, the convening of a special children's court as described.

The remaining concern of the Bulger trial was the boys' sentence of the juvenile equivalent of life imprisonment with an expectation of their having to serve at least eight years. On a conviction of murder the judge at the trial had no alternative but to pass sentence as he did. Thus no consideration at the trial could be given to the background, needs and rehabilitation of the boys concerned. The overall consideration in such an automatic sentence is one of appropriate punishment in preference to a care programme in an attempt to rehabilitate them. Rather than the prospect of residential care in secure accommodation throughout their childhood, a more sensible programme of care might have been a package of residential and specialised foster care.

A children's court or special children's court as suggested for Scotland should be enabled even in cases of murder committed by a child to arrange a sensible package of care and supervision of the child and to have it reviewed on a regular basis.

ENDNOTES

1. Children (Scotland) Act 1995, sections 43(3), 51(3), 51(11), 54-56(4)(6), 57-60, 65(1), 67, 73 and 76-80 and schedule 1, para. 3.

2. Lockyear, Andrew and Wilkinson, David, *Citizens Serving Children*, Scottish Office 1992, page 5 and *Children and Young Persons Scotland* (1964), Edinburgh, HMSO 1995, para. 252, recommendation (15). (The Kilbrandon Report).

3. Scottish Office, Social Work Series, Statistical Bulletin: *Referral of Children to Reporters and Children's Hearings 1994* (No. SWK/CH/1995/15), Government Statistical Service, 1995 para. 9.

4. Social Work (Scotland) Act 1968, sections 42 and 49 (repealed).

5. Criminal Procedure (Scotland) Act 1975 sections 168 and 364.

6. *O v Rae* (1st Div.) 1993 SLT 570J and 574I

7. *Kennedy v F* (2nd Div.) 1985 SLT 22

8. *D v Kelly* (Extra Div.) 1995 SLT 1220.

9. *McGregor v L* (2nd Div.) 1981 SLT 194.

10. Norrie, Kenneth K., *Children (Scotland) Act 1995* (Greens Annotated Acts), W. Green/Sweet and Maxwell page 36/51, Edinburgh 1995.

11. *Scotsman* newspaper 4 and 25.11.93 and 28.1.94.

Chapter 5

Children's Rights:
The United Nations Convention
on the Rights of the Child (1989)
and the Children's Panel System

Children's Rights: The United Nations Convention on the Rights of the Child (1989) and the Children's Panel System

5.1 Respect for children's rights

A child being more vulnerable than an adult demands that children's rights must be regarded with the utmost seriousness. All children require proper care and protection.

Daily at children's hearings panel members are all too aware of difficulties children find themselves in. Grounds or reasons for referring children to hearings emphasise the appreciation of the negative experiences of some children. No child deserves the fate of being the victim of abuse, suffering neglect or lack of parental care. A child should be protected from the disasters of his or her own making in the consequences of his or her committing offences, truanting, abusing - solvents, drugs or alcohol - or being beyond parental control. The right of the child to be protected from harm is the business of the children's panel system. Put positively the child has the right to be properly cared for and protected.[1]

The Scottish children's panel care philosophy should find its justification in the principles enunciated in the United Nations Convention on the Rights of the Child, which proclaims that 'childhood is entitled to special care and assistance' and recognises that 'the child for the full and harmonious development of his or her personality should grow up in a family environment in an atmosphere of happiness, love and understanding'. Panel members are all too painfully aware that many children have anything but a happy childhood lacking a satisfactory family environment. A child has the right to a happy childhood.

The clear principles outlined in the U.N.Convention on the Rights of the Child should not be considered as a vague idealism to be achieved sometime in a utopia, but what every child has a right to expect. These principles could be viewed as a series of compromises as highlighted by the Spanish reservation regarding the recruitment of children above the age of 15 years for military service. The convention could be considered as representing a minimal standard of what every child is entitled to expect.

5.2 The United Nations Convention on the Rights of the Child: a standard of measurement

If Scottish children, as children anywhere, are entitled to expect as minimum rights, the rights outlined in the U.N. Convention on the Rights of the Child, the question has to be asked as to whether or not the law in Scotland relating to the care of children and the children's panel system in particular is delivering what should be expected even in relation to these minimal rights. Unfortunately the answer on occasion has to be in the negative, although it may be otherwise on other occasions.

The most obvious example of not affording to children even minimal rights, which are enjoyed by adults, is found in respect of what is tolerated in the care of children by their parents. Children are the only persons within the U.K. devoid of an absolute protection in law from assault. They are discriminated against in any deed, which would otherwise be considered as an assault if committed against an adult, so long as the deed is committed against them by their parents under the guise of reasonable parental chastisement.[2] For the state to allow corporal punishment to be inflicted on children by their parents could be argued as being contrary to the convention.

In contrast on a positive note, the Children (Scotland) Act 1995 is mindful in some respects but not others of the provisions of the U.N. Convention on the Rights of the Child of 'the family as the fundamental group of society and the natural environment for the growth and wellbeing of all its members and particularly children'. The role of parents in this context is crucial. The Act begins in a practical way by defining that role. The responsibility of the parent is to 'safeguard and promote the child's health, development and welfare' as well as giving 'direction' and 'guidance to the child'. If a parent lives apart from the child the parent is expected to 'maintain personal relations and direct contact with the child on a regular basis'.[3] This statement of parental responsibility is helpful both to children's reporters and hearings in relation to children referred to them as to when compulsory supervision is necessary.

The logical sequence to the description of parental responsibilities and rights within the Children (Scotland) Act 1995 should have been a statement of the same for children. Children's responsibilities could have been described as including respect for parents in their reasonable exercise of their responsibilities and rights, regular attendance at school if of school age and responsible behaviour in the community taking into account their age and maturity. Children's rights should have been defined as including the rights of children to life, protection from avoidable harm or injury, a sound upbringing in responsible parenting and access to health and education resources to be afforded the opportunity to fulfil their potential as adults. Children's responsibilities and rights encapsulated in a brief statement within the Act would have more effectively promoted in Scotland the aims of the U.N. Convention on the Rights of the Child.

Failure to take the opportunity to include a succinct statement of children's rights within the Children's (Scotland) Act 1995 could be said to reveal less than a full commitment in Scotland to the desire effectively to promote children's rights.

5.3 The effort to promote children's rights within the children's panel procedure

Panel members and children's reporters may argue that at least every effort is made within the procedures of the children's panel system to guarantee children's rights.

The relationship between the lay amateurism and legal professionalism within the structure of the children's panel system helps to create a proper respect for children's rights. The lay children's hearing in subjecting children to compulsory supervision are aware that their decisions may in turn on appeal be subjected to the scrutiny of the sheriff, the sheriff principal and the Court of Session. Children's reporters are well aware of the potential challenge for proof in the sheriff court in any formulation of statement of grounds. Hearings are at pains to explain to families the substance of reports submitted to them and to encourage children in particular to express their views.

The insistence on a proper standard of proof, of facilitating appeals against decisions for compulsory supervision, the expression of the views of children at children's hearings being encouraged and the justification of any decision at a hearing or by the sheriff as the welfare of the child throughout childhood being paramount certainly equates with international standards.

The best interests of the child being the justification of a children's hearing decision prior to 1995 has been sacrificed in favour of any decision of a hearing or sheriff being based on the welfare of the child being the paramount consideration. However even this basis is somewhat weakened.

It is also further weakened by the qualification of that standard in that 'for the purposes of protecting members of the public from serious harm' the children's hearing or the sheriff would be justified in basing their decision on criteria not necessarily consistent with the child's welfare. The dilution of the principle of the decision as being justified primarily on the best interests of the child even in the exceptional circumstances of the child being a serious threat to other persons is contrary to Article 3 of the U.N. Convention on the Rights of the Child.

The situation of a decision by a children's hearing or sheriff being justified on the notion that the child was at serious risk to others, whilst at the same time there was not justification of the decision primarily on the child's welfare is in any case unrealistic. If the child was thought of as being a serious threat to others on account of, for example, his or her offending behaviour or being beyond parental control, it would clearly be in the child's best interests in order to best assist the child in the improvement of his or her behaviour to be subject to compulsory supervision.

Perhaps on a more positive note the use of safeguarders demonstrates a desire to better promote children's rights within the children's panel system. A children's hearing or the sheriff can appoint a safeguarder for the child if it is considered necessary in the child's interests. The assumption is that the child's interests would not otherwise be properly protected. In each local authority council area there is a list of safeguarders of, for example, solicitors and social work or other child care professionals. The expectation is that the safeguarder provides a report to the hearing or the sheriff to highlight what he or she considers is best for the child. In researching the report the safeguarder may try to befriend the child to win the child's confidence so as to understand the child better. In addition the safeguarder is provided with copies of reports provided to the hearing or the sheriff and may discuss the reports with their authors. The report of the safeguarder can provide to the hearing or the sheriff a useful insight into the child's predicament.

5.4 Legal representation at children's hearings

Legal representation is rare at children's hearings as most families could not afford the services of a solicitor. The child and parent each have the right to be accompanied by a representative at the hearing, although the representative need not be a solicitor. In recent years in the experience of the author, if a representative is present, the representative is invariably a solicitor.[4]

Legal aid is unavailable to families attending children's hearings but available at sheriff court proceedings on proofs and appeals. Lack of legal aid to facilitate representation in one forum cannot be justified on its availability in another forum, as lack of fairness in one forum cannot be rectified by fairness in another. Under the present system more affluent families, who can afford legal representation at hearings, have an unfair advantage.

At any children's hearing there is the possibility, albeit remote in most hearings, of the child's liberty being an issue. The hearing may issue a warrant or renew a warrant or child protection order to send a child to or keep a child in a place of safety temporarily. Later a hearing may require a child to be on compulsory supervision ordering the child to stay with a foster parent (carer) or be in residential care. With such a possibility of loss of liberty, legal representation should be considered as essential at all hearings.

Lack of effective legal representation for most families at children's hearings is contrary to Article 37(d) of the U.N. Convention on the Rights of the child. The British government ratified the convention subject to certain qualifications including the position as described in respect of Scottish children's hearings. Legal aid should be made available to children and their parents at hearings as it is in the sheriff court in order to effectively facilitate legal representation.

The regular attendance of solicitors representing children at children's hearings would result in an effective monitoring and implementation of children's rights independent of the children's panel system itself. On a positive note it would demonstrate to the public that the children's panel system took the issue of children's rights seriously.

There are occasions when a family feels vulnerable at a children's hearing. They may feel powerless not only on account of the reasons for their presence expressed in the children's reporter's statement of grounds but their awareness of power lying with the three panel members at the opposite side of the table. They need the support of a solicitor to give a sense of protection in a redress of the power balance. Regardless of their financial circumstances a family should have the effective option of having a solicitor, if they so wish, by the provision of legal aid.

If solicitors were in attendance at all children's hearings the three lay panel members might find themselves at some disadvantage and in some difficulty. The children's hearing upgraded to a children's court

61

with a children's judge sitting with two panel members would be much more able to cope with the presence of solicitors at every hearing. Children's judges would be able to ensure that children's rights at hearings were properly respected.

5.5 Exclusion of adolescent teenagers in the main from the children's panel system

Effectively for the children's panel system the child is a child of any age up to his or her 16th birthday. A few older teenagers remain within the system if they happen to be on supervision on their 16th birthday and for so long as they remain on supervision to a children's hearing. They are considered as children until such time as their supervision is terminated. No-one can remain on compulsory supervision beyond his or her 18th birthday.

Young people of 16 and 17 years of age committing offences, if prosecuted, would appear in an adult court. If the young person is still on compulsory supervision to a children's hearing, the sheriff would be obliged to ask the hearing for advice or remit the case for disposal. If the sheriff court so wished, it could similarly act regarding a young person of that age not on compulsory supervision.[5]

For the majority of older teenagers the situation of the 16 and 17 year old young person is unsatisfactory. This is particularly so for such a young person, who has recently experienced the philosophy of care of the children's panel system.[6] This philosophy appears in some respects to be left behind at the children's hearing. All young people of 16 years and over, with very few exceptions, committing offences are dealt with within the criminal justice system and treated in effect as adults.[7] The transition between the children's panel and the criminal justice systems for the young person can be quite difficult. The Scottish Child Care Law Review Group in 1990 recognised this difficulty in their suggestion of the desirability of further consideration to be given to the needs of young people between the ages of 16 to 21 years in conflict with the law.[8]

The suggestion of a further review or research on how young people 16 to 21 years of age in trouble are to be dealt with should be welcomed. Yet young people of 16 and 17 years of age should not be considered as part of a wider age group of those 16 to 21 years of age. Rather they should be considered in accordance with Article 1 of the U.N. Convention on the Rights of the Child (1989) in terms of the definition of the child as a 'human being below the age of 18 years unless the law applicable to the child, majority is attained earlier'. In other words it could be argued that they should be dealt with within the children's panel system as children, perhaps adapting the system to accommodate their particular needs.

Again the suggestion might be that 16 and 17 year old offenders could be dealt with by children's reporters and children's hearings upgraded to children's courts with a children's judge assisted by two panel members.

REFERENCES

1. UN Convention on the Rights of the Child 1989 (CM1976), London, HMSO, Preamble and Articles 1, 3, 6, 9, 19, 27-29, 34, 35, 37(d), 38-40 and Spanish and UK reservations.

2. Children and Young Persons (Scotland) Act 1937 section 12(7).

3. Children (Scotland) Act 1995, sections 1, 2, 6, 15(1), 16, 39, 51, 52, 60, 61 and 64-69.

4. Children's Hearings (Scotland) Rules 1986 rules 11 and 19.

5. Criminal Procedure (Scotland) Act 1975, sections 372 and 373.

6. Scottish Office: *Scotland's Children: Proposals for Child Care Policy and Law* (CM 2286), Edinburgh, HMSO 1993, paras. 7.28-7.30.

7. Scottish Association for the Study of Delinquency: *Offenders 16 to 18: Report of Working Party 1993*, para. 2.3.

8. Scottish Office: *Review of Child Care Law in Scotland*, Edinburgh, HMSO 1990, paras. 22.1 and 22.5, recommendation 87.

Chapter 6

A Solid Foundation for Care:
Grounds Firmly Established

A Solid Foundation for Care: Grounds Firmly Established

6.1 The need for grounds established

In any consideration of children's rights, a child, as indeed any person, has the right to be protected from false allegations.[1] Considered negatively, the children's reporter's statement of grounds should to his or her best endeavours and in good faith be supported by sufficient evidence. The right to challenge grounds, or have grounds tested if the child cannot understand the explanation, should ensure that a children's hearing decision for compulsory supervision at least has the ingredient of a proper basis of concern, namely that the grounds are based on accepted or proved events.[2]

To emphasise that grounds must be established, or accepted by the family as being the truth, appears to be stating the obvious. The whole business of building a concern for the need of a child for compulsory supervision is that allegations made in respect of a child are provable. In other words there should be, as the Orkney Inquiry report suggests, 'solid evidence to justify the course'.[3] Thus compulsory supervision as an expression of care has to be firmly based.

In Scotland the children's panel system has experienced within the five years from 1990 to 1995 the reality of such a proposition in what could be considered as the tragedies affecting seventeen children from seven families in Orkney and South Ayrshire. Allegations of sexual abuse concerning the children were in the final analysis unable to be proved. The element of tragedy in part related to the children being separated from their parents for significant periods of time. Following allegations of sexual abuse all of the children under emergency procedures were removed to places of safety. In the case of the South Ayrshire children they were later made subject to compulsory supervision and required to reside outwith their families.[4] The nine Orkney children were separated from their parents for slightly in excess of one month, whilst the South Ayrshire children suffered a period of separation of nearly five years.

In order to gain an understanding of the lessons to be learnt from these tragedies the reader has to have some knowledge of what happened to the seven families. Although the general issue of unprovable allegations is the same, other related and sometimes different issues arose.

6.2 The Orkney story

The account of what occurred in Orkney will be kept as brief as possible consistent with the general issue already referred to. The Orkney story focuses on what happened to nine children from four families in the island of South Ronaldsay.[3] They were alleged to be victims of 'organised sexual abuse', yet they themselves had not made any complaint of being abused. Seven of the children denied they had been sexually abused. The remaining two children gave no indication that they had ever been sexually abused or witnessed it.[5]

The story begins on 6, 12 and 13 February 1991, when during 'disclosure therapy' three children of one family alleged that organised sexual abuse of children took place on the island of South Ronaldsay, implicating nine children from four other families as victims and/or observers.

These three children, who made the allegations, had themselves previously been victims of sexual abuse and were from a family, which had a history of serious sexual abuse. The three children concerned were in foster care on the Scottish mainland.

On 26 February 1991 the sheriff at Kirkwall in Orkney granted authority to remove the nine children from the four families in South Ronaldsay from their homes to places of safety on petition of a social worker.

On 27 February 1991 from about 6.50 to 7.30 am in the island of South Ronaldsay in a joint police-social work operation the nine children from the four families were removed from their homes. Later on the same day they were flown from Orkney to places of safety on the Scottish mainland. The parents initially had no idea where their children had been taken to nor were they allowed access to them.

After the arrival of the children on the Scottish mainland, the children were medically examined but 'no positive evidence' was found of sexual abuse.

Following the removal of the children from their families to places of safety three children's hearings were held in March 1991, the principal hearing being that of 5 March 1991. At the hearing the parents rejected the children's reporter's statement of grounds detailing the allegations of sexual abuse. The children were not present at the hearing. The hearing instructed the children's reporter to make an application to the sheriff for proof. In their consideration that the children had been taken to places of safety, the hearing decided to issue warrants to detain the children in places of safety.

At the proof hearing in Kirkwall sheriff court on 3 and 4 April 1991 the issue of the truth or otherwise of the allegations of organised sexual abuse was not, nor has ever since, been determined. The sheriff discharged the grounds for a reason other than a determination of the facts. His attitude was that the children's hearing procedures had been 'fatally flawed' due to the absence of the children from particularly the hearing of 5 March 1991. Later the children's reporter appealed against the sheriff's decision to the Court of Session. During the Court of Session proceedings the intention of the children's reporter to abandon the grounds was intimated even if the appeal were decided in his favour. In the event his appeal was decided principally in his favour. Later he abandoned the grounds.

Due to public concern regarding the Orkney events, a judicial inquiry sitting in public in Kirkwall in Orkney, was set up by the government on 20 June 1991.

As to whether or not the allegations of organized sexual abuse were true was outwith the remit of the inquiry. However the parents and others, who may feel themselves accused by the allegations, according to the Orkney Inquiry report, 'remain entitled to rely on the basic presumption of innocence'. Perhaps that presumption of innocence should determine our attitude to the allegations.

The abandonment by the children's reporter of his statement of grounds means that in fact the allegations are withdrawn. It is not without significance that no adult was ever prosecuted in respect of the allegations of sexual abuse. In any case the nine children did not claim to have been sexually abused and 'no positive evidence' on medical examination was found of sexual abuse.

It would have been quite a different story in Orkney if the allegations had been proved. Without the foundation of provable allegations any action taken to protect children will come to naught.

6.3 The South Ayrshire story

The South Ayrshire story commenced about nine months earlier than the Orkney events, yet its conclusion was to some extent influenced by what had occurred in Orkney. What occurred in South Ayrshire as compared even to Orkney was clearly 'a tragedy of immense

69

proportions'. This was principally due to an enforced separation of the children from their parents for almost five years on account of allegations finally adjudged to be untrue.

This story started in June 1990, when eight children from three closely related families were removed from the care of their parents and taken to places of safety. It was alleged that they were victims of sexual abuse or were of the same family as children suffering such abuse. The children were referred to children's hearings by the children's reporter as requiring compulsory supervision.

In August 1990 the sheriff found the grounds of sexual abuse proved. A children's hearing in due course on the basis of established grounds imposed compulsory supervision, requiring the children to be in care living apart from their parents. On various occasions on reviews of their supervision requirements later hearings continued the same or similar arrangements.

Regardless of the sheriff and the children's hearing in 1990 believing that the children had been sexually abused or at risk of sexual abuse, the Court of Session in 1993 ordered a retrial of the sexual abuse allegations, which according to correct legal procedure within the children's panel system as outlined in the Social Work (Scotland) Act 1968 had been proved three years earlier. On 6 December 1993 the retrial under a different sheriff began.

The Court of Session decision to in effect order the retrial of these allegations was a significant milestone in the history of the children's panel. The circumstances of the case were deemed to be 'extraordinary','unforeseen' and 'exceptional'. In persuading the court to order the retrial references were made on behalf of the parents to the experience of or lessons to be learnt from Orkney. It was also suggested that the court should be mindful of similar lessons to be learnt from the English experience of Cleveland and Rochdale, which will be referred to later in this chapter. The parents claimed to have 'obtained additional expert evidence'. This evidence coupled with the lessons learnt from Orkney, Cleveland and Rochdale might cast a different light on whether or not the allegations were true.

The Court of Session had no alternative but to order a retrial of the allegations in the exceptional circumstances, which prevailed in this case. If there was any possibility of reasonable doubt as to the truth of the allegations, even after they have been judicially judged to be true, that doubt must be explored.[6] Provision is now made in legislation under appropriate circumstances for grounds established previously by the sheriff to be reheard.

In an appropriate understanding of the evidence during the retrial, ordered by the Court of Session, the children's reporter was unable to prove his case. Thus the grounds found to have been established almost five years earlier were declared in February 1995 to be unproved. Arrangements were to be made for the return of the children in a phased programme to the care of their parents, whom they had not lived with for nearly five years. By October 1995 it was reported to the Court of Session that all the children had been successfully reunited with their parents.

6.4 English experience of unprovable child abuse allegations

What occurred in Scotland in the tragedies of Orkney and South Ayrshire should not be considered as necessarily endemic to the children's panel system, but can occur regardless of legal structures. Similar tragedies have occurred in both Cleveland and Rochdale within appropriate English legal procedures.

According to the Cleveland Inquiry report 'in total 125 children were diagnosed as sexually abused between February and July 1987' in the Cleveland area. Allegations of sexual abuse principally arose from a medical diagnosis due to 'the presence of physical signs . . . elevated from grounds of 'strong suspicion' to an unequivocal 'diagnosis' of sexual abuse'. The consequences were self evident in that allegations, if relying solely on such medical diagnosis as described, would be unable to be proved.[7]

Twenty children from six families in Rochdale were made wards of court in 1989 because of allegations of sexual abuse. The majority were removed from their families to places of safety to reside with foster parents (carers). It was claimed that 'they had been subjected to or were at risk of satanic or ritual abuse by adults'. In the final analysis the judge 'held that the case for the satanic and ritual abuse of the children had not been made out'.[8]

6.5 A determination to learn from experience

There is a determination in Scotland to learn from the experiences of Orkney, South Ayrshire, Cleveland and Rochdale. The deliberations of the Orkney Inquiry was to some extent influenced by what had occurred in the two English tragedies. Likewise the deliberations of the

Court of Session in respect of the South Ayrshire case was not only influenced by what had happened in England but also in Orkney.

In the crises of all of these tragedies, when initially these allegations came to light, children in what was thought of as emergency situations were taken to places of safety. In Scotland legislation has ensured that in these kind of emergencies the sheriff will only grant a child protection order for the removal of the child to a place of safety if he or she 'is satisfied that there are reasonable grounds to believe' the allegations being made in respect of the child relative to the way in which the child is being treated or neglected or any risk of the child being harmed. To convince the sheriff the applicant attempting to persuade the sheriff to grant the order has to 'state the grounds' and produce 'supporting evidence'. In other words the sheriff even at this early stage would have to believe that there is adequate evidence to back the allegations even before any direction by a children's hearing to direct the children's reporter to make an application for proof on exactly the same grounds.

It is unfortunate that the legislators by-passed the children's hearing in respect of issuing child protection orders. The reason must be that they did not have the confidence in the hearing to be able properly to scrutinise applications for such orders. The hearing is the natural forum for the consideration of the presentation of a distressing family crisis with sensitivity away from a busy sheriff court routine. If the hearing were upgraded to a children's court, the children's judge along with two panel members would be well able to consider issues relating to child protection orders away from the adult court.

The need to ensure that in referring a case to a children's hearing the children's reporter has adequate evidence to prove his or her statement of grounds, containing the allegations, has been re-emphasised in being made explicit in legislation. To achieve this aim and avoid similar tragedies to what occurred in Scotland in Orkney and South Ayrshire all children's reporters should be solicitors. The ability of the children's reporter to prove his or her grounds in respect of the child, exercised in good faith, is the least that the children can expect and is their right.

ENDNOTES

1. UN Convention on the Rights of the Child 1989 (CM1976), London, HMSO 1992, Article 40.

2. Children (Scotland) Act 1995, sections 57, 65, 68 and 85.

3. *Report of the Inquiry into the Removal of Children from Orkney in February 1991*, Edinburgh, HMSO 1992, particularly paras. 1.3, 1.10, 2.21-99, 4.30, 5.21, 5.25, 5.51, 6.73, 6.96, 7.11-21, 9.6, 11.1-25, 12.1-35, 14.60-101 and 14.107. (Orkney Inquiry Report)

4. *Scotsman* newspaper 6.12.93, 28.2.95 and 18.10.95.

5. *Sloan v B* (1st Div.) 1991 SLT 530.

6. *L, Petitioners* (No.1) (1st Div.) 1993 SLT 1310; *L, Petitioners* (No.2) (1st Div.) 1993 SLT 1342.

7. *Report of the Inquiry into Child Abuse in Cleveland 1987* (CM214) London, HMSO 1988; particularly page 2, para. 12; page 6, para. 12; page 21, para. 64; page 36, para. 2.1; page 44, para. 2.52; and page 243, paras. 3 and 7. (Cleveland Inquiry Report)

8. *Rochdale Borough Council v A* (1991) 2 FLR 192; *Rochdale Borough Council v A & others:* September 1991 (Family Law), pages 374 and 375.

Chapter 7

The Principles and Application of
Care Through Social Education

The Principles and Application of Care Through Social Education

7.1 The theme of care

Taking children's rights seriously leads inevitably to a regard for their welfare. The two concepts of rights and welfare are inter-related. It could be argued that rights arise from a concern for the welfare of the child. This concern for children's rights pre-supposes a philosophy of care.

In the children's panel system the common theme is one of care. The Kilbrandon report emphasised that regardless of the child's trouble, care was to be applied. Children committing offences were entitled to care as much as children having suffered abuse or neglect.[1] The emphasis on care was incorporated into legislation, but by 1995 was unfortunately somewhat diluted.[2]

A proper insistence on care in the children's panel philosophy could be summarised in the assertion that the welfare of the child is paramount. If the philosophy is ignored, to use a seafaring analogy, the children's panel system would be like a ship adrift without an anchor.[3] The insistence on the child's welfare being paramount should be the principal characteristic of the children's panel system rather than the procedures of that system. It is a principle worth maintaining but it must be properly understood. The principle that the child's welfare is paramount sounds idealistic. The idealism has to turn into practical actions.

7.2 The meaning of the word 'care' for children's hearing and parent

The word care principally suggests worry, anxiety, concern and caution. Those who represent the community as panel members on children's hearings have to be worried, anxious and concerned for these troubled children, whose cases they will have to consider at hearings.

Yet care by it's definition has a feeling otherwise it ceases to be care. It should have a compassion. The care of a parent for a child is not

77

cold and calculating, but should have a sense of warmth. Although the Spanish word *carino* is not the same as the English word 'care', even although it may look like it, it gives the flavour of a good environment where care flourishes in a good home. *Carino* expresses love, affection, fondness, liking and tenderness towards the child.[4] Unless the parent loves the child, is fond of or has tenderness towards the child, it is unlikely that the parent can be caring by being at appropriate times worried, anxious, concerned and cautious for the child.

The English word 'care' and the Spanish word *carino* bring together the idea of care exercised with feeling of a responsible parent. Thus it is care as should be exercised by a responsible parent that underlines the meaning of care in the children's panel system.

7.3 Responsible parental care the measure of care

Society demands that parents exercise responsibility towards their children. The Children (Scotland) Act 1995 sets out what is expected of a parent in caring for a child. At the most basic level the parent has the duty 'to safeguard and promote the child's health, development and welfare'. A parent would also be expected 'to provide in a manner appropriate to the stage of development of the child direction and guidance to the child'. Children would normally be expected to live with their parents. However where a child was not living with a parent the responsibility is on the parent 'to maintain personal relations and direct contact with the child on a regular basis'. These responsibilities would only be expected of a parent where it was 'practicable and in the interests of the child'. In order to carry out their responsibilities parents are accorded rights, which in normal circumstances include the right 'to control, direct or guide, in a manner appropriate to the stage of development of the child, the child's upbringing'.

The three panel members and parents at the children's hearing must share a common understanding of care if dialogue at the hearing is to yield results. Their understanding of care should be that of the exercise of responsible parenting. Parental child abuse or neglect could be seen as a disregard of the parental duty to safeguard and promote the child's health, development and welfare. A child truanting or committing offences, for example, may be regarded as a child being in need of proper direction and guidance. Being beyond parental control is self-evident in the parent's failure or inability to control the child. The common endeavour of both the panel members and the parents at the hearing is in essence to ensure that the child in trouble is afforded a proper upbringing. The responsibility of the hearing is to insist that the child has that opportunity hopefully with parental co-operation, but if necessary despite the lack of it.

7.4 Supervision a vehicle of care for child in trouble

To ensure that a child is cared for and given a proper upbringing the children's hearing imposes a supervision requirement if such supervision should be on a compulsory basis. The children's reporter, in not referring a child to a children's hearing, may arrange with the social worker that the child should have the benefit of voluntary supervision. Supervision in such terms is a vehicle to channel the care which the troubled child may require in order to improve if necessary the quality of his or her upbringing.

The definition of 'care' in the repealed Social Work (Scotland) Act 1968 and 'supervision' in the Children (Scotland) Act 1995 are almost identical, referring to protection, guidance, treatment and control of the child.[5] These features of care or supervision encapsulate the parental responsibility for the upbringing of children. The context of parental responsibility would suggest that care is almost synonymous with supervision. In other words care is conveyed through the parent's supervision of the child.

Given the child's problems both the children's reporter and the children's hearing in their respective roles have to ask whether or not the parents' supervision and care of the child is adequate for the child's proper upbringing. If not the child requires more not less parental supervision. The parents may require supervision in order that they themselves might be encouraged to supervise their child in order to care for their child properly. Neither the children's reporter nor the hearing have any power over parents. However the reality is that an indirect power is apparent over parents as exercised in respect of their children. Parents are well aware that the hearing have the ultimate power to deprive them of having the child within their own home.

The social worker's role, if possible, is to oversee the parents' supervision of the child to ensure that the child is properly cared for, namely care as expected to be exercised by a responsible parent. The social worker will give advice and encourage the advice to be acted upon by the parent. The social worker will try to encourage the parent to exercise his or her own supervision of the child in a satisfactory way, so that the child's problems may be overcome. The effectiveness of social work supervision is not to take over from the parent, but to enable the parent to be a responsible parent to better help the child in difficulty.

Where the child, as a result of the children's hearing decision, is no longer in the physical control of his or her parents for the time being, someone else on a daily basis substitutes for the parent, either a foster parent (carer) or residential care professional. Even in such difficult circumstances the social worker and others try to prevent the parent feeling shut out from the care of the child. The care of the child in foster or residential care is to be thought of as a partnership between the foster parent (carer) or residential staff and the parent working together to assist in the supervision of the child, provided such involvement is not contrary to the child's best interests.[6]

The concept of supervision within the children's panel system is of supervision built on top of supervision. The parent caring for the child in trouble should have the principal task of supervision, but the social worker must oversee that supervision to ensure that it is satisfactory, enabling the parent to tackle the child's problems.

7.5 Supervision as a method of social education

In supervision, whether compulsory or voluntary, the social worker supervises the parent, for the parent properly to supervise the child. At the same time in partnership with the parent the social worker will have contact with the child to seek as appropriate to exercise some influence for good. All children, whether in trouble or not, require parental supervision in order to experience a good upbringing. What therefore is the special ingredient required for social work supervision of a child in trouble? The extra ingredient is summed up in two words 'social education'.

The idea of social education has hardly been taken seriously. Often the impression is created that the social worker's responsibility is solely social work input, whilst schools deal with education. The Kilbrandon report never envisaged social work and education as being apart. The report recommended a social education department within a local authority area and not as happened two separate departments of social work and education. The test in assessing the case of the troubled child would be the 'child's needs for special educational measures'.

The concept of social education was ill-defined or developed within the Kilbrandon report. The only hint is given in the attempt to justify why those requiring care and protection and delinquent children should be dealt with within the same forum of the juvenile panel. They both need education in 'its widest sense'.

Before describing the need for education within the concept of social education, it is better to consider what is suggested by the word 'social'. It gives the clue as to what education is to address. The word 'social' identifies the problems. The grounds or reasons drawing the child to public attention relate frequently to social malfunctioning of relationships, either within the family itself or in the local community. Child abuse, neglect, lack of parental care or the child being beyond parental control, point to poor relationships and often the denial of care within the family. Anti-social behaviour or delinquency or truancy indicate the child's difficulties within wider relationships in the community. The abuse of solvents, drugs or alcohol by the child tells of the child's distress within him or herself or with the world in general, including both family and community.

Solutions have to be found for these troubles highlighted by the children. The solution is education, but education in it's widest sense. In addressing these problems in supervision, the social worker and other child care professionals along with the parents have to implement what was thought of by the Kilbrandon Report as 'special measures of education and training'.

Keeping in mind the pre-occupation for the child in trouble is the malfunction of relationships, it is better to begin with the child in the family to which 'special measures of education' have to be directed. The Kilbrandon report insisted on the child's home life being taken seriously. Its strengths had to be built upon so that 'the natural influences for good within the home and family' were strengthened. In this way the parents would be properly supported to give the child 'sound and normal upbringing'. Parental rights relate to the responsibility of the parent for the child's upbringing. The Kilbrandon insistence on strengthening family life stresses that social education is not only for the child but for the family, in order to assist the child in trouble so as to achieve a 'sound and normal upbringing'. The issue is in fact the correlation of social education with achieving a 'sound and normal upbringing'.

The very ground of referral in respect of a child indicates the possibility of a lack of soundness or normality in the child's upbringing. The sound and normal upbringing must relate to the responsible exercise of parental rights and responsibilities. Parents have to be re-educated within the framework of social work supervision to exercise their rights over their children responsibly.

81

7.6 Multi-agency assistance for social education

The Kilbrandon term 'social-education' implies a multi-agency approach in every endeavour to assist a child in trouble.

Multi-agency approach to tackle children's problems is not only apparent in the submission of a variety of reports to children's hearings but in the presence of professionals from different agencies at hearings. In most cases of school age children social workers and guidance teachers are present at hearings. Health visitors would normally be present when cases of pre-school children are discussed at hearings, due to health visitors' regular contact with some families of children under the age of five years. If necessary, dependent on the circumstances of the case, other professionals, for example, a psychologist or a psychiatrist, may be involved.

The children's hearing itself in particularly difficult cases may request a joint assessment from child care professionals from different agencies, even although some of them may not have so far been involved in the child's case. The hearing can insist on a multi-agency assessment by requiring the child to 'attend or reside at any clinic, hospital or other establishment' for a period not exceeding 22 days for the purpose of further investigation. The practice of allowing the child to remain at home rather than require the child to reside elsewhere during the period of multi-agency assessment is increasing. Multi-agency community based assessment if at all possible is much to be preferred.

The philosophy of care implemented as social education at it's most basic indicates that no one group of child care professionals or agency has the monopoly of wisdom in assessing children's needs or the ability alone to assist children in trouble. The concept of social education implies of necessity multi-agency co-operation.

7.7 Best interests of the child and the public interest

Social education by means of supervision is an attempt to endeavour to ensure a proper upbringing for the child in trouble, who may not otherwise be afforded it. To endeavour to ensure a proper upbringing for the child is to try to achieve what is in the best interests of the child in accordance with international standards.

In considering the best interests of the child by definition in the use of the adjective 'best', the clear implication is that the best interests of

82

the child is to pursue what is to the child's best possible advantage. Another way of expressing the same idea is to insist on the welfare of the child as the 'paramount consideration'.

The grounds of referral in the reverse illustrate in essence what may be to the best possible advantage of the child. In a good upbringing it is to the best advantage to a child to experience the love and care of parents free from the threat of any harm or neglect and to be influenced by parents to be of good behaviour, to take advantage of education and to be able to achieve his or her full potential. For this to happen the child 'should grow up in a family environment, in an atmosphere of happiness, love and understanding'. Day by day at children's hearings panel members are well aware that many of the children appearing before them have anything but a happy childhood. They are faced with the challenge of making decisions for these children in promoting their welfare to their best possible advantage so as to try to achieve for them a happy childhood, which otherwise would elude them.[7]

Promoting the best interests of the child in insisting on the welfare of the child as paramount is in the public interest. The problems of children as described in the variety of grounds, whenever they arise, are not in the public interest. Children's hearings acting to protect abused or neglected children are seen to be acting in the public interest. Even hearings trying to resolve the difficulties of children, who fail to attend school properly, abuse solvents, drugs or alcohol or are out of control can be seen to be attempting to act for the public good.

Difficulty arises in an apparent conflict between the best interests of the child and the public interest in the children's hearings considering cases of children who are anti-social in their behaviour to the extent of their committing offences. Perhaps public interest demands that the delinquent children should be punished with the punishment fitting the crime and not having their welfare considered as paramount. To consider their cases in terms of their welfare in the context of their upbringing is to go beyond the superficial notion of punishment. The hearings have the obligation to explore perhaps the underlying reasons for their offending. These reasons could well reveal deficiencies in their upbringing. For the hearing to try to overcome these difficulties by, for example, compulsory supervision, reveals an effort to improve the quality of their upbringing, that is of their care. The public interest is served by such an effort.

To deal with the difficult scenario of the child, who may be a threat to public safety, by retreating from the principle of best interests of the child in terms of the welfare of the child being paramount is mistaken.

Within the concept of the decision by the children's hearing based on the welfare of the child being paramount, there is ample justification for a child, perceived as a threat to public safety, being on compulsory supervision.

In the final analysis any child in trouble is a member of the public as any other child. To promote that child's best interest in considering the child's welfare as paramount by definition is in the public interest. The desire of the children's hearing is that the quality of the child's upbringing will be improved. To facilitate the desired improvement, supervision may have to be imposed in care expressed through social education. If the desired improvement for the child in trouble is achieved, the public interest is well served.

ENDNOTES

1. *Children and Young Persons Scotland* (1964), Edinburgh HMSO 1995, paras. 13, 35, 140, 233 and 252(40). (The Kilbrandon Report)

2. Children (Scotland) Act 1995, sections 1(1), 2(1), 16(1) and (5), 52(2)(3), 56(4)(b), 69(3) and 70.

3. *Report of the Inquiry into Child Care Policies in Fife*, Edinburgh HMSO 1992, page 76, para. 11. (Fife Inquiry Report)

4. Collins Spanish Dictionary (2nd Edition) 1988, 'carino'.

5. Social Work (Scotland) Act 1968 (repealed), section 32(3).

6. Skinner, Andrew, *Another Kind of Home: A Review of Residential Child Care*, Scottish Office, Edinburgh, HMSO 1992, page 59, paras. 3.6.1-3.6.5. Scottish Office: Scotland's Children: Proposals for Child Care Policy and Law (CM 2286), Edinburgh HMSO August 1993, para. 3.25.

7. UN Convention on the Rights of the Child 1989 (CM 1976), London, HMSO 1992, Preamble and articles 3, 6, 9, 24, 27, 28, 29 and 31.

Chapter 8

Voluntary and Compulsory Supervision

Voluntary and Compulsory Supervision

8.1 The choice between voluntary and compulsory supervision

It may seem that the most crucial decision taken by a children's reporter is whether or not to refer a child to a children's hearing in the belief that the child requires compulsory supervision. This is a misconceived view. The crucial nature of the decision is taken at a stage earlier. The children's reporter has to decide whether the child and/or parent requires social education in view of the trouble the child is in and information about the child and his or her background as given in reports. If the child and/or parent requires social education in order to afford to the child a sound upbringing, the children's reporter has then to decide whether or not within social work supervision it be delivered on a voluntary or compulsory basis.

In 1993 in Scotland 40,503 referrals of children thought to require compulsory supervision were made to children's reporters. A third of referrals were referred by children's reporters to children's hearings in their belief that the children required compulsory supervision. In comparison only 10 per cent were referred to social workers for voluntary supervision.[1]

8.2 Negative arguments against compulsory supervision in favour of voluntary social work supervision

The arguments in favour of voluntary social work supervision could be contrasted as negative and positive with the two aspects having equal appeal. Voluntary supervision to convey social education could be said to be preferable to the alternative of compulsory supervision, on the assumption that social work supervision is necessary for the child in trouble and/or indirectly for the parent in order to ensure a responsible upbringing for the child. Thus the alternative to be avoided is the imposition of compulsory supervision. The negative anti-compulsory supervision argument is to begin with appealing.

Less to do with compulsory social work supervision itself, is the actual process of having it put in place. If compulsory supervision is thought to be necessary, the children's reporter has to refer the case to the children's hearing. Regardless of the desire and practice to have the proceedings of hearings held in private with the minimum number of persons present, the fact is that the hearing is a public forum. The public are present as represented by the 3 panel members. The public forum aspect is made more obvious if on a few occasions the press are present.[2]

The child and parent, in being summoned to the public forum of the children's hearing, could be said in a sense to be stigmatised especially if it results in the child being placed on compulsory supervision.[3] Regardless of how kind and considerate the panel members at the hearing try to be, the family may feel humiliated and embarrassed by the experience. For them the hearing deciding on compulsory supervision compounds their humiliation and embarrassment. Parents may feel that they somehow or another have failed in their responsibilities.

8.3 Positive arguments in favour of voluntary social work supervision

The principal positive argument in favour of voluntary social work supervision is simply enshrined in the word 'voluntary', suggestive of free will. The teacher/student relationship analogy is most obvious in the student, anxious and willing to learn, benefiting from education. If the family can be persuaded to accept voluntary social work supervision and be co-operative, the chances of success are far greater. The lessons of social education transmitted through social work supervision will be learnt and progress in the care of the child through a sound upbringing will be better achieved.

In rejecting the idea of imposing sanctions directly on parents, the Kilbrandon committee were of the view that the social worker best assisted the family on the basis of 'persuasion and co-operation'. Indeed they went as far as to claim that the idea that parental co-operation with the social worker to aid the child could be achieved by 'compulsive sanctions' was 'fundamentally misconceived and unlikely to lead to any practical and beneficial result'.[4]

A parent or a child voluntarily accepting social work supervision and co-operating with the social worker is more motivated to make a success of it than would be the case if supervision were imposed compulsorily.

8.4 Arguments for compulsory social work supervision

In describing the benefits of voluntary supervision, there seems little chance that compulsory supervision will be effective. Yet on 30 June 1993, 10,227 children subject to compulsory supervision to children's hearings in Scotland amount to 8.9 children per thousand of the population.

The children's reporter having decided to refer the child to a children's hearing, or the hearing itself having determined, in agreement with the children's reporter, to impose compulsory supervision in order to force the family to accept social education, the question has to be asked as to how compulsion is to work. The proposition is that the family have to be forced to accept social education, compelled to care for the child properly or instructed to give the child a sound upbringing.

Compulsion rather than persuasion can be decided upon only when there is no viable alternative. To bring together compulsion and social education is an act of desperation. It should be used only to a minimal extent as intended by the Kilbrandon report. In fact the children's hearing or sheriff is prohibited from making a requirement or order in respect of a child unless the hearing of sheriff considers that 'it would be better for the child that the requirement or order be made than that none should be made at all'.

The reason for this desperation in trying to force the family to accept social education relates to persuasion not being an option, the seriousness of the child's troubles and the need for the local community to keep an interest for the time being in the child.

Within the children's panel system compulsion implies that the family should be accountable to the local community for the sound upbringing of the child in insisting on parents carrying out their responsibilities towards the child properly. The community as represented by the three panel members at the children's hearing have to be satisfied that social education is being properly received by the child and/or parent. This implies that the social worker and other child care professionals involved in the child's case are also responsible to the local community for their part in delivering social education by means of compulsory supervision. The reporting back to the hearing is of course done at the stage of the review of the child's supervision requirement. Being accountable to the community is part of the force being used on the family through compulsory supervision to submit to social work supervision. The family know that should they fail other sanctions are available to the hearing, inclusive of the possible removal of the child from home or if the child were required to reside away from home, the continuation of that state of affairs.

If compulsory supervision is imposed by the children's hearing in conveying social education to the child and/or parent, the social worker and other child care professionals involved in the case would be acting on the authority of the local community. In a radical reform of the children's panel system the upgrading of the children's hearing to the children's court, with the introduction of a children's judge as chairman of the hearing, would give an additional force to the authority of the local community. It would add an authority to what the panel members were advising and doing for the child. It might even be persuasive in having the advice ultimately accepted by the child and/or parent to improve the child's upbringing.

To turn away from the child in trouble due to an anticipation of the family's lack of credible co-operation would be unacceptable to any society. The local community through the three panel members at the children's hearing has against the odds to endeavour to do something for the family in order that the child has the chance of being offered a sound upbringing. Not to provide the child and/or parent with social education would be a betrayal of any philosophy of care for troubled children. Compulsory supervision ensures that the child in trouble, even in the most difficult circumstances, is not to be abandoned by the local community.

Compulsory supervision by order of a children's hearing is a public statement even to the child or parent unwilling to recognise it, that certain manifestations of the child being in trouble are unacceptable to the local community. At its most draconian in the removal of the child from the parents' care, the message is made clear that certain behaviours or attitudes are intolerable and the local community has the will to deal with the matter. Such is not vengeance or punishment, but at it's extreme is a clear statement that regardless of difficulties, the child will be afforded social education to be given the chance of proper care and upbringing.

8.5 Need for the child to be removed from home

If compulsory measures of care were necessary the Kilbrandon report envisaged that in most cases such care would be afforded to the child whilst the child remained at home. Only in a minority of cases would the child require to be removed from home and only for a 'limited period'.

90

A children's hearing, ordering that a child reside elsewhere than the family home, may appear somewhat at odds with the children's panel care philosophy. The care within the philosophy is modelled on the experience of the care of a parent in the proper upbringing of a child. To take away a child from the care of a parent is almost a denial of care itself. Perhaps it could be described as the step of despair for the family. A child at least for the moment is better away from the family. For a short period on a day to day basis the care of the parent will be replaced by the care of the foster parent (carer) or residential care staff.

Even although the child is removed from home, other than it being contrary to the child's welfare, every effort will be made to keep contact between the child and the parent. The care of the child in foster or residential care should, as far as possible and sensible, be a shared partnership between the foster parent (carer) or residential care staff and the parent.[5] As gradually the parent takes the greater share in the partnership, the aim of the foster parent (carer) or residential care staff will be achieved in the return of the child home, with the assurance that progress made in care will be continued at home.

Before a child is removed from home by a children's hearing, careful consideration has to be given as to why such a course of action is absolutely necessary. There should be a consensus as to the factors which singly or accumulatively indicate the need for such a drastic step. The factors would not necessarily be the same for all cases due to the differing circumstances of each case.

Removal from home may be necessary where there is a loss of control. The parent may have lost control either of him or herself or of the child. Loss of control relates to a breakdown of relationship between the parent and child. As evidenced in serious child abuse cases, the parent may well have lost control of him or herself, so that the children's hearing may decide that for the time being the parent should not be having control over or responsibility for the child. The loss of control may be indicated by grounds specifically relating to the child's being beyond parental control, for example, in running away from home or behaving at home in an unruly and disruptive way.

For the child to be properly controlled or cared for an alternative environment may be required for the child other than the child's home or even community. The child cannot sensibly remain within the family. If the child were to continue to reside at home his or her upbringing may remain unsatisfactory. The lack of control or care within a family concerning a child is not resolved by ignoring the problem. Abuse or neglect or at the other extreme the child remaining beyond control, despite well meaning support from child care professionals, may simply continue. The hearing may be driven to the conclusion that the child would not be properly cared for unless removal of the child from the family takes place.

The most extreme expression of the children's hearing's anxiety, that a child be controlled, is not simply to require a child to reside in a children's home or residential school, but whilst there to be liable to be placed in secure accommodation. In Scotland there are seven residential establishments with secure accommodation, providing 84 places with an occupancy rate of about 90 per cent.

The legal criteria allowing a children's hearing to order that a child sent into residential care and be liable to be detained in secure accommodation relates strictly to the child's previous record of absconding, the likelihood of the child's absconding and the risk to the child whilst absconding, or alternatively the likelihood of the child injuring him or herself or others if not placed in secure accommodation. It seems utterly inconsistent with a care philosophy, but the dilemma faced by the hearing is simply that if the child is not available to be cared for, other than being placed in secure accommodation how can the child be cared for?

Anxiety as to whether a parent can properly behave as a parent may be persuasive of the need to remove a child from home. The parent may simply be unable to accept or exercise responsibility for the child. Care and protection cases are the obvious examples of such inability. The parent simply cannot be trusted to exercise his or her responsibility properly. Less obvious may be the case of parents, who in a sense have given up in despair in relation to their children's behaviour of recidivist delinquency, which they are unable to influence, or being beyond their control.

Children may require to be removed from home at a much earlier stage than the children's hearing insisting that the child be subject to compulsory supervision. The earlier stage might relate to emergency circumstances following allegations of the child being abused or neglected. Even in these circumstances the feeling rightly exists that removal of children from home should be only a last resort. In this context the sheriff, or a justice of the peace in the sheriff's absence, would only grant a child protection order to remove the child to a place of safety if he or she believed that the child was 'suffering significant harm' or would suffer such harm if not removed to a place of safety. Alternatively the alleged abuser of the child might be excluded by order of the sheriff from the child's home rather than the child be removed from home. If there was a suspicion of abuse the sheriff could issue an assessment order where, for example, the parents were not prepared to co-operate with the authorities in the investigation of that suspicion. The aggregate of these three orders is a desire to respect the family in minimising the necessity for the removal of children from home even in emergencies to circumstances where there is no real alternative.

In an unsatisfactory home life or upbringing the child may need the experience of foster or residential care. The aim would be that the experience would afford to the child at least temporarily a proper upbringing. So long as it is consistent with the child's best interests this temporary experience of a proper upbringing outwith the family home has to be transformed into a permanent one as soon as possible within the child's own home. This requires the preparation for the child to be returned home to be accomplished in partnership with the parent. Only in this way would the benefits of social education continue once the child is returned home.

8.6 Contracts within compulsory care arrangements

Within the framework of compulsory supervision the concept of contract might be suggested. Children's hearings would be urged to negotiate a contract with the family indicating in some detail what is expected of parents and children during the period of compulsory supervision. The contract document is intended to be linked to the statement of reasons of the hearing imposing compulsory supervision.

The attraction of the concept of a contract is that it would spell out what was expected of the family by the children's hearing. At the same time within the context of compulsory supervision the children's hearing would have at least some statement of intention by the family for their co-operation to achieve a better standard of upbringing for the child. If the family were unwilling to enter into a contract an alternative might be for the hearing to draw up a statement of expectations for improvement. They could easily do so by making greater use of conditions, which can be part of a supervision requirement. Later at the review of the supervision requirement the hearing would have the opportunity to assess whether or not targets for the child's supervision had been achieved.

ENDNOTES

1. Scottish Office, Statistical Bulletin, Social Work Series, *Referral of Children to Reporters and Children's Hearings*, 1993 (No. SWK/CH/1994/18), Government Statistical Service, December 1994, para. 6.2.

2. Children (Scotland) Act 1995, sections 1(1), 2(1), 16(3), 39(5), 43, 52(a) and (d), 55, 56, 57-61, 65(1)(a), 69(1)(c), 69(11), 70, 73 and 76-80.

3. *Report of the Inquiry into Child Care Policies in Fife*, Edinburgh HMSO 1992, page 98, para. 24. (The Fife Inquiry Report)

4. *Children and Young Persons Scotland*, Edinburgh HMSO 1995, paras. 13, 17, 21, 35, 127, 140, 161 and 167. (The Kilbrandon Report)

5. Skinner, Andrew, *Another Kind of Home: A Review of Residential Child Care*, Scottish Office, Edinburgh, HMSO 1992, page 59, paras. 3.6.1-3.6.5 and page 67, para. 3.8.2 and Scottish Office: *Scotland's Children: Proposals for Child Care Policy and Law* (CM 2286), Edinburgh, HMSO 1993, paras. 3.43, 7.13-7-15 and 7.18-7.19.

Chapter 9

A Snapshot of the Daily Life of the Children's Panel: Fife Child Care Inquiry

A Snapshot of the Daily Life of the Children's Panel: Fife Child Care Inquiry

9.1 The nature of the Fife Child Care Inquiry

The Fife Inquiry lasted over three and a half years. the Inquiry was set up on 1 March 1989 under the chairmanship of Sheriff Brian Kearney. This was the longest British child care inquiry. It's report of some 780 pages was published on 27 October 1992, the same day as the Orkney Inquiry Report. In contrast to the Orkney Inquiry, the Fife Inquiry was held in private. Unlike the Orkney Inquiry the Fife Inquiry did not arise from any child abuse allegations, which might have caught the attention of the media. Naturally as a consequence, it gained little publicity. The Fife Inquiry has almost become the forgotten inquiry.

Forgotten or not, there is much to learn from the Fife Inquiry, particularly with regard to fundamental, philosophical issues. The Fife Inquiry was concerned with the day to day life of the children's panel system and is therefore worth studying. It provides a snapshot of the daily life of the children's panel.

The Fife Inquiry report describes a number of cases of children, victims of child abuse or lack of parental care, children truanting from school and recidivist offenders. Arising from a study of these cases, philosophical issues were discussed in the report, not in a rarified atmosphere of theory but in a practical way. The philosophy became in a sense existential. The debate as to the need for or type of supervision arose from the consideration of actual children's case experiences. Thus the Fife Inquiry report provided a snap-shot in time of the daily life of and issues faced by the children's panel in a part of Scotland of a population of about 350,000.[1]

9.2 The events of the Fife Child Care Inquiry

To understand the philosophical debate which took place during the Fife Inquiry and the snap-shot of the children's panel system provided by their report, some knowledge of the events of the Fife Inquiry is necessary. It is not the purpose of this chapter to give a summary of the inquiry report. The summary of events will be kept as brief as possible.

Fife Regional Council approved it's one page social work department's care in the community child care policy on 26 November 1985. The document was circulated to social workers, advising them that the policy should be considered as a 'benchmark' for their work with children in trouble.

The policy direction of principally care in the community for troubled children was welcomed. Troubled children are best assisted in their own homes and communities. Only as a last resort, when community options were inappropriate, should a child be received into foster or residential care. However, within four years of the approval of the care in the community child care policy characterised as emphasising care in the community, an inquiry was under way.

In 1988 two advisers from the Scottish Office (Social Work Services Group) undertook a case study of 20 children recently sent by Fife children's hearings into residential care. From a study of these cases the advisers made some observations about how child care in the community policy in their view was being implemented. They warned against the fear of social work stigmatising being pushed too far. The role of the children's hearing should be properly recognised. Residential care should be considered in a positive way. The advisers' report shadowed many of the conclusions of the Inquiry report.

9.3 Fife Child Care Inquiry findings

The social work child care policy of care in the community for children in trouble was not adversely criticised. What was wrong, according to the Fife Inquiry, was how it was put into practice.

Although the Fife Inquiry report was critical of the way in which child care policy of care in the community relative to children in trouble was implemented, such a criticism should not be considered as applicable solely to Fife prior to the Inquiry. It is a criticism which could be relevant anywhere else or at any time in the practice of social work.

The Fife Inquiry claims that it detected an orthodoxy associated with the practice of policy. The word 'impetus' was used to express the same idea, suggestive of the idea of stimulus, that is what makes one do something to overcome any resistance. Orthodoxy is in the religious world correct belief as opposed to and intolerant of heresy. Used as a metaphor, according to the Inquiry, orthodoxy existed within social work practice in Fife.

Thus in Fife, according to the Fife Inquiry report, there was an orthodoxy linked to an impetus, giving the orthodoxy a force whereby the correct belief was to be enforced. Other views of the practice of social work were presumably to be set aside. The correct belief was motivated by a fear of stigmatising families. Not to stigmatise a child or family was in the child's best interests. To stigmatise a child was obviously the converse of best interests.

What is meant by stigmatising a child or family? In the ancient world slaves or criminals were branded possibly with a hot iron, whereby they would bear a mark instantly recognisable pointing to their demeaning status in society. The metaphor translated into modern social work practice was that any person, including a child in trouble, who had a social worker formally assigned to his or her case, was possibly stigmatised. The idea of stigmatising was taken further in a belief that such social work involvement with the family whether voluntary, or even more so compulsorily, was 'potentially damaging'.

Thus the belief that social work intervention in the life of a child or family was possibly stigmatising, with the degree of stigmatisation depending on the extent of that involvement, was in essence the orthodoxy which was said to give impetus or stimulus to social work practice in Fife.

Perhaps this fear of stigmatising by social work contact is seen clearly in what could be described as a social work ladder of stigma. Each of the various degrees of social work involvement or 'hierarchy of preferences', ranging through different types of social work assistance such as voluntary supervision, compulsory home supervision, the more drastic compulsory foster supervision and the worst of all compulsory residential care supervision, could be depicted metaphorically as rungs of a ladder. Voluntary supervision would of course be the bottom rung of the ladder, whilst residential care was at the top.

The orthodox social worker in Fife, as portrayed by the Fife Inquiry report would, to use the metaphor of the ladder of stigma, avoid the child in the first place getting on to the ladder. There would be no question that the child would be stigmatised if the child were not on the ladder in the first place.

If the child were on the ladder at all the social worker would endeavour to keep the child as low on the ladder as possible. The worst fate of all which could befall a child was to be sent into residential care, which was sincerely believed by some to be damaging to the child.

The implication of the Fife Inquiry findings regarding the social work belief in stigma, is that the fear of stigma was exaggerated to such an extent as to prejudice how children, who might require social work help, should best be assisted.

A caricature of the way in which the care in the community child care policy was implemented in Fife is succinctly described. It was suggested to the Inquiry that 'the official interpretation' of policy could be 'paraphrased' as 'a family situation is, will and always will be best for all children at all times'.

With such simplicity perhaps it would not be surprising that judgements about how to best assist children in trouble, could be reached with a certain predictability.

The orthodoxy, coupled with the fear of stigmatising as expressed in the implementation of social work policy in Fife of care in the community, was viewed as over-simplistic by the Fife Inquiry. It was also suggested that the policy was applied rigidly.

9.4 Criticism of the Fife Child Care Inquiry's findings

The concept of orthodoxy or stigmatisation used as vehicles of criticism by the Fife Inquiry report is open to question.

Historically orthodoxy has sometimes been characterised by fanaticism and intolerance. Professional work has to be informed by what could be described as beliefs, or if belief is too strong, the word assumption. Within the children's panel system the philosophy of care should be shared by all involved. Having a philosophy implies what could be described as acceptable or unacceptable beliefs or assumptions. Once one differentiates between the two, the result is the emergence of an orthodoxy or at least the notion of a consensus. Thus orthodoxy is almost inevitable in any professional practice based on an acceptable philosophy, which dictates good pratice. Perhaps what the Fife Inquiry has identified is an orthodoxy which was too simplistic, narrow and rigid.

Regardless of what the Fife Inquiry report says, stigmatisation is a problem. For any self-respecting and sensible parent appearing before a children's hearing for his or her child's troubles, the experience must be on occasion one of embarrassment and shame. Equally a family may very well have the same feeling in having a social worker assigned to them by order of a hearing.

Although stigmatisation in many cases is almost inevitable, it should not be exaggerated or be disabling of social work. It should not necessarily be assumed that to have a social worker assigned to the family should be avoided because it is thought to be stigmatising. In any case any thought of social work involvement being stigmatising may be overcome by an acceptance by families that such involvement is both necessary and helpful.

If one avoided the use of the word stigma in the metaphor of the ladder, what is left could be referred to as the ladder of preferred social work options or 'minimum feasible intervention', a phrase which the Inquiry claimed to have 'coined'. According to the Inquiry this phrase of 'minimum feasible intervention' meant 'a policy of adopting the least invasive form of intervention seen to be practicable'.

'Minimum feasible intervention' as a concept in itself is to be commended. It conveys a reasonable impression that social work intervention should be kept to a minimum in the lives of families of children in trouble, no more than is absolutely necessary. What appears to be implied by the Inquiry report in the use of this concept was of less social work help being provided to the troubled child than the child actually needed.

Endemic in both the idea of the ladder of social work stigma or minimum feasible intervention, is the hierarchy of social work resources from voluntary social work supervision to compulsory residential care. If a policy is being applied in a simplistic, rigid or mechanical way, the obvious danger is that the hierarchical ladder becomes a fixture, whereby in all cases a lower resource precedes a higher resource, 'creating a tariff of favoured disposals with an over-mechanical preference for the lower tariff'.

Thus it might be thought that a child should not be in compulsory residential care unless compulsory foster supervision had been tried and failed, not on compulsory foster supervision unless compulsory home supervision had been tried and failed, or not on compulsory home supervision unless voluntary social work supervision had been tried and failed.

If the social work resources were viewed simplistically as climbing a ladder, rigidity would soon become the order of the day. However, there is still an element of truth that of course there is a hierarchy of social work support ranging from the informal to the intensive, from voluntary support to compulsory residential care. Setting aside simplicity and rigidity, it is still possible to have a hierarchy of resources but to be used sensibly to fit each child's needs.

9.5 The child's welfare is paramount: The Author's submission to the Inquiry

Any child care policy statement should have an explicit assertion, such as that 'the welfare of the child was paramount', recognising the objective of pursuing the best interests of the child. Without such an explicit assertion 'policy objectives good in themselves . . . become ends in themselves'. Perhaps a seafaring analogy best describes the effects of such omission as 'a policy 'adrift without an anchor''.

A policy direction of care for children in trouble in the community deserves support. Families if at all possible should be kept together as long as possible, so long as it was safe. If the children were required to be sent to live with foster parents (carers) or reside in residential schools or children's homes, they should do so only for as long as was absolutely necessary. However, these excellent ideas of care in the community, enshrined in a policy statement considered outwith the proper context of the explicit assertion that the child's welfare is paramount, become ends in themselves.

The positive merit of an explicit assertion in the care in the community child care policy for troubled children, of the welfare of the child being paramount, is that the policy objectives are for the child focussed properly. The hierarchy of social work resources and preferences are well enough known. In implementing the policy with the reminder continually in the forefront of the child's welfare being paramount, the social worker is better able to assess and match the child's needs with the particular resources within the hierarchy.

For those working with troubled children, a child care policy should not be considered as 'operational instructions'. Children in trouble should not 'be treated as 'cases' or according to rigid rules'.[2] In implementing a child care policy, rightly emphasising care in the community, the test is not what is a dictated preference necessarily, but what is best for the individual child in the child's own unique circumstances of trouble and background. For most children in trouble, of course it will mean care in the community and hopefully resources can be developed to make such an option more attractive and effective for even more children. The policy will serve the child, not the child be fitted into the policy.

Such a thesis of the consequences of the absence of an explicit assertion of the child's welfare being paramount within the care in the community child care policy statement of 1985 is credible in the Fife experience as highlighted in the Scottish Office advisers' report. Thus considering policy objectives without the reminder of the child's welfare being paramount, resulted in equating the objectives with the best interests of children. This could lead to a distortion of the practice of policy. Such a mistake can only be avoided by focussing on the child in order to consider his or her welfare as paramount in each individual case.

9.6 Philosophy of care - welfare and rights

The Fife Inquiry report went some way to accepting the author's thesis of the need to an explicit assertion of the child's welfare being paramount in a child care policy statement. The report, in paraphrasing some of the sentiments and rights as expressed in the UN Convention on the Rights of the Child 1989, recommended that in any future statement there should be in essence an assertion of what each child is entitled to expect as of right in a good family life and upbringing in order to develop to full potential,[3] as well as declaring that should there be 'conflict with the rights of any other person, the child's rights are paramount'.

One can equally assert that the child's rights are as paramount as that of welfare. Rights arise from welfare as indeed welfare could be considered as arising from rights. This is seen clearly in the preamble of the UN Convention on the Rights of the Child 1989. Even before the enunciation of articles defining the rights of children, it is clear in the preamble of the Convention on the Rights of the Child that such rights are based on certain assumptions in essence of welfare. They include special consideration which should be extended to children as well as the assertion of children being entitled to experience a happy family life.

The argument in favour of rights arising from welfare is that the child's rights are derived from society's concern for the welfare of children. The focus should always be on the child and thus on the child's welfare, rather than necessarily what is derived or implied in a recognition of the child's welfare, namely the children's rights.

The desire to promote the welfare of children creates the insistence that children have rights, which must be taken seriously.

Whether talking about welfare or rights, in any consideration of policy the child comes before the policy, not the child fitting into the policy. In this way the focus is correct so that desirable objectives of any care in the community child care policy can be seen in perspective. Without the insistence of the child's welfare being paramount explicitly stated, the distortion in the implementation of policy becomes too apparent.

The achievement of the Fife Inquiry is that it reasserted a proper balance within the children's panel system between policy and practice in a re-affirmation of rights and welfare. The policy must be subservient to and informed by the philosophy of care. The reality is children in trouble and how they are to be best assisted. The snap-shot

103

is that of the Fife children's panel endeavouring to achieve what they considered to be in the best interests of children. At children's hearings panel members were determined to insist that their decisions reflected their concern for the welfare of children.

ENDNOTES

1. *Report of the Inquiry into Child Care Policies in Fife*, Edinburgh HMSO 1992, particularly pages 3 and 4, paras. 10-13, page 76, para. 11, page 78, paras. 2 and 3, page 125, para. 10, page 131, paras. 32 and 33, page 132, para. 36, page 181, para. 3, page 182, para. 5, page 183, para. 7, page 193, para. 42, page 572, para. 3, page 585, para. 2, page 588, paras. 18-21, pages 589-590, paras. 23-25, page 615, para. 23, page 617, para. 8 and page 623, para. 24. (The Fife Inquiry Report)

2. Scottish Office: *Scotland's Children: Proposals for a Child Care Policy and Law* (CM 2286), Edinburgh, HMSO August 1993, paras. 2.6 and 2.18.

3. UN Convention on the Rights of the Child 1989 (CM 1976), London, HMSO 1992, preamble and articles 6, 12, 13, 19, and 24.

Chapter 10

The Scottish Children's Panel and Europe

The Scottish Children's Panel and Europe

10.1 Recognition for the children's panel system in Scotland

In a quarter of a century of its existence the children's panel system has established itself as a unique feature of Scottish life. The Children (Scotland) Act 1995, although in some measure diluting the children's panel philosophy of care in responding to the experiences of Orkney, South Ayrshire and Fife, still retains some of the tradition of that philosophy. Perhaps that tradition was too strongly entrenched in the implementation of the Social Work (Scotland) Act 1968 from 1971 to 1996 to allow it to be easily eclipsed.

The philosophy and practice of care, described as supervision, despite setbacks, is the strength and resilience of the children's panel system. This strength is the conviction that local communities should take responsibility for children in trouble in their midst insisting on a proper exercise of parental responsibility. The contribution made by lay panel members, representing local communities at children's hearings in caring for children in trouble, is recognised and will continue. The relationship between the hearing and the sheriff court, the sheriff principal and the Court of Session should have ensured a proper balance between lay justice and legal professionalism. Unfortunately that balance has been tilted too far in the direction of the courts, so as to cause genuine anxiety for the standing of hearings. Only radical reform can remove that anxiety.

Radical reform of the children's panel system is necessary. The upgrading of the children's hearing to a children's court with a children's judge sitting with two panel members is required. A children's court would more effectively recognise children's rights in Scotland in conformity with the U.N. Convention on the Rights of the Child 1989, for example, to insist on legal representation of children at children's hearings.

10.2 The European dimension

Child care professionals involved in assisting children in trouble in European countries outwith the U.K. with no experience of lay justice may find some difficulty in understanding and accepting the concept of the community taking responsibility for the care of these children in their midst. They would be right in arguing that to take the difficult decisions of judgement regarding children in trouble demands not only an element of professional training but standing, if those who sit in judgement on children are to be properly respected by the community. The introduction of the children's judge to the children's hearing might satisfy that demand.

In Scotland the powers granted to the sheriff to in effect rehear the case and substitute his or her own decision for that of the children's hearing on an appeal from a hearing demonstrates a profound distrust of hearings by those, who legislated in the 1995 Act.[1] This distrust would be overcome with the introduction to hearings of children's judges yet retaining the valuable and proven contribution of lay panel members sitting with judges in the consideration of the children's cases. In towns and villages throughout Scotland this proven contribution by panel members has been recognised. Panel members have had a task of considering at children's hearings difficult problems in a sensitive and effective manner as presented to them by families.

The suggestion of a children's judge sitting with two lay panel members at a children's hearing or court in Scotland would at least be similar to the practice in Germany of at least in the second or third level of the juvenile court dealing with juveniles over 14 years of age, of a professional juvenile judge sitting with two lay judges or two or three professional juvenile judges sitting with two lay judges. It would also make the Scottish children's panel system much more acceptable to those similarly involved in other parts of Europe in juvenile justice.

The philosophy and practice of care expressed through supervision, is by no means unique to the Scottish children's panel system, but is characteristic of other systems of justice to be found elsewhere outwith the U.K. in Europe. It is not the system of justice or procedures that matter, but the attitude to children in trouble, which informs and motivates practice.

Over 40 years prior to the Kilbrandon report of 1964 the concept of social education was expressed in German legislation. The *Reichsjugendgerichtsgesetz* (RJGG: 'Juvenile Court Act') of 1923 favoured the idea of education rather than seeking vengeance for the child's misdeeds. The same idea is again expressed in the *Kinder und Jugendhilfegesetz* (KJHG Children and Youth Care Act) implemented in

1991, emphasising voluntary support for parents in their co-operation to assist the child. Parents might need the assistance of child care professionals with children in trouble to support them in the proper upbringing of their children.[2] Thus the German concept is akin to the Scottish in emphasising good upbringing as the core of the idea of social education.

In France in quite a different system of justice for children as expressed through the activities of the children's judge or magistrate *(juge des enfants)* the concept of caring for children in trouble and helping families is uppermost in intention. The children's judge endeavours to reach an understanding with parents on how best to help the child in trouble. A solution to the child's problems is negotiated with the family. The children's judge deals with care and protection cases referred by O.S.E. *(Oeuvre de Secours aux Enfants)* or delinquent children referred by the public prosecutor. The age of criminal responsibility in France is 13 years. Court social workers implement the judge's decisions if treatment or supervision is required *(liberte surveillee)*. Essentially the task undertaken is to enlist the co-operation of the parent to assist the child in the spirit of a caring philosophy.[3]

Unlike the quite separate concerns and responsibilities of the youth court and the family proceedings court in England and Wales it is interesting that the French children's judge like the Scottish children's hearing deals with a wide spectrum of children's problems not solely confined to delinquency, sharing the same attitude of exploring the needs of the child and seeking the co-operation of the parent. Similarly in Germany children under 14 years not subject to the criminal law, regardless of their problems causing public concern, would be dealt with by family courts.

The realisation that children's problems cannot be compartmentalised is appreciated not only in Scotland but elsewhere in Europe. In contrast in England and Wales there is a split between civil and criminal concerns regarding children in trouble. The youth court will deal with children 10-13 years and young people 14-17 years inclusive who commit offences. The family proceedings court will deal with civil concerns. It is a distinct feature of the Scottish system that both children's reporters and children's hearings have to deal with a wide range of problems of care and protection to delinquency.

Where there is a split between civil and criminal a possibility of bridging the gap is revealed in an interesting example. The age of criminal responsibility in Switzerland is seven years.[4] Even although there is a distinct division between the criminal and civil concerns

109

relating to children, on occasions these concerns do come together and have to be resolved not in separate forums but in the same forum. Children, who offend, would be dealt with by the local federal juvenile penal judge. Care and protection cases such as abuse or neglect would be the responsibility of the local guardianship board of the commune, where the child was deemed to be resident. If the juvenile judge was dealing with a case of a child involving issues relating to the child committing an offence as well as manifesting issues of care and protection the juvenile judge would deal with all of these problems. The guardianship board of the commune would be content to allow the juvenile judge assume what would have otherwise been its responsibility.

The co-operation of the parent in an endeavour to help the child in trouble cannot be emphasised enough. In Scotland the children's reporter is able to divert children away from children's hearings by arranging voluntary supervision in a programme of care for the child of social education being confident that the family will co-operate.

In the Netherlands and Belgium reliance on and confidence in parental co-operation on a voluntary basis is demonstrated in difficult circumstances of child abuse in a very effective way. The Dutch confidential doctor bureau (Vertrouwensarten), piloted in 1972 and extended throughout the Netherlands by 1976, is a partnership between paediatricians and other child care professionals in helping families where children are said to be victims of abuse. The co-operation of the family will be enlisted to ensure the safety and well-being of the child. The understanding between the bureau and the family is that the abuse ceases immediately. If the abuse is admitted, treatment including social work support will be offered to the family. If the abuse is not admitted the matter will be referred to the Child Protection Board, which may in turn initiate care proceedings or report the matter to the prosecutor. Most families accept the voluntary help offered by the bureau. This approach has to some extent been copied in Belgium in Child in Distress (Kind in Nood) and SOS Enfants in Flemish and French speaking areas respectively.[5]

10.3 The European Convention on Human Rights 1987

Apart from the U.N. Convention on the Rights of the Child 1989, the European Convention on Human Rights, predating the U.N Convention by two years, is the only effective measurement by which the Scottish children's panel system can be appropriately made accountable for respect of children's rights in the European context alongside other systems of dealing with children in trouble. Children are as much entitled to enjoy the rights described in the European Convention as adults. Indeed it could be argued that they are entitled being children to a greater protection in terms of their rights than adults.

Children and their parents in any country adhering to the European Convention have the right to seek redress in the proper implementation of these rights as guaranteed by the Convention, but only after they have exhausted every legal remedy available in their own country. The European Commission and the Court of Human Rights in Strasbourg are the means whereby remedies can be sought.[6] In this way it could be argued that the European Convention is more effective than the U.N. Convention on the Rights of the Child by the mere fact the former provides an effective vehicle of complaint, whereby the latter is reliant on the willingness of the state to properly implement. Thus the Scottish children's panel system has to be sensitive to any infringement of the European Convention.

During the time in the Spring of 1991, when the nine Orkney children, separated from their parents, were required to reside with foster parents (carers) or in a residential school, correspondence sent by parents to them were interfered with in contravention of Article 8 of the European Convention.

Following the Orkney and South Ayrshire experience steps were taken to avoid suggestions, that Scottish children's hearing procedure might be in violation of the European Convention, particularly in respect of removal of children from their homes say in emergency circumstances arising from allegations of their being abused or neglected or fear that they might be further abused or neglected. The removal of children from their homes in these or other circumstances should only be considered according to the Convention by a 'competent legal authority'. The Children (Scotland) Act 1995 now insists on a close surveillance by the sheriff court in procedures relating to the child protection order.[7] An upgraded children's hearing to children's court would be a much more appropriate forum.

Not to allow full access by a mother to the reports provided to a children's hearing or to the sheriff on appeal against a hearing's decision has been found by the European Court of Human Rights to be in violation of Article 8 of the European Convention as impairing the right of the mother to a fair hearing and in violation of her ' right to respect' for her private and family life'.[8] The findings of the Commission have been accepted by the government, which had already indicated an intention to amend the law to impose a duty on

111

the children's reporter to inform the family of their right to see copies of reports to the hearing or the sheriff except in circumstances where to do so would be against the child's interests.[9] It would be much more sensible if parents as of right received copies of all reports made available to hearings as they already receive copies of children's reporters' statements of grounds.

It is odd that the European Court of Human Rights does not regard, despite the government's argument to the contrary, the Scottish children's hearing even as a tribunal for the purposes of Article 6 of the Convention regarding it only as an adjudicatory body. The court felt that panel members were not sufficiently independent 'from the administrative authorities' due to the way in which they are appointed or removed from office. This issue will have to be addressed urgently so that panel members participating in hearings are regarded by the court as independent. In Scotland they are certainly not regarded as other than independent. The attitude of the European Court to the hearing is reason enough for consideration of the upgrading of the hearing to children's court.

10.4 The future of the Scottish Children's Panel in Europe

The future of the Scottish children's panel system is inextricably bound up with that of Europe. With closer European ties engendered by the European Union gradually other systems of care and justice for children in trouble will begin to have some influence. For too long the Scottish system has appeared to remain in a backwater with insufficient recognition elsewhere in Europe and insensitive to outside influences.

Considering that what the children's panel system had to offer in Scotland for children in trouble during 25 years was both child-centred and compassionate, perhaps Scots could be excused from feeling a bit disappointed that no other country sought to replicate it in dealing with children in trouble in any significant way. The retreat in part from the radicalism of the Kilbrandon vision of the children's panel system and its practice for a quarter of a century in the implementation of the Social Work (Scotland) Act 1968 as manifest in the Children (Scotland) Act 1995 is another disappointment.

In overcoming disappointment and attempting to recover the Kilbrandon radicalism in a determination to practice the philosophy of care, perhaps those involved in the children's panel system would do well to look beyond their own system to other systems outwith the U.K. in Europe. The radical reform of the children's panel system in the

112

upgrading of the children's hearing to a children's court would not only bring the Scottish system more into line with other systems on the continent, but assist in the reclaiming of the Kilbrandon vision of philosophy and practice of care towards children in trouble. The two panel members, sitting with the children's judge during the hearing, would retain something of the community taking responsibility for these children.

The European Convention on Human Rights 1987, particularly in the judgements of the Court of Human Rights in Strasbourg, will at least ensure that the European dimension in Scotland is taken seriously.

The Children (Scotland) Act 1995 at least ensures that the Children's panel system will survive but radical reform is necessary. Within the Scottish system of assisting children in trouble child care professionals should continue to practice the philosophy of care in the spirit of the Kilbrandon report of 1964 in terms of 'the needs of the individual child as the test for action'.[10]

In Scotland the determination for the community through the children's panel to care effectively for children in trouble has proved itself in the past and will prove itself in the future, insisting by word and deed in dealing with children in trouble that the welfare of the child is paramount.[11]

ENDNOTES

1. Children (Scotland) Act 1995 sections 50(3)(5), 52(2), 56(4)(b) and 57-60.

2. Lorenz, Walter, *The New German Children and Young People Act*, British Journal of Social Work (1991) 21, pages 329-339.

3. Tonkin, Boyd, *A Bench without Tears*, Community Care Magazine 14.7.88; Philpott, Terry *Crime and Punishment*, Community Care magazine 24.10.91; and Neate, Polly, *A Different Way of Working*, Community Care Magazine, October 1991, pages 15-17.

4. Booth, Tim (ed.), *Juvenile Justice in the New Europe*, ch. 1, Dünkel, Frieder, 'Legal Differences in Juvenile Criminology in Europe: Social Services Monographs - Research in Practice 1991'.

5. *The Kingdom of the Netherlands Facts and Figures: Justice 1989*, chapter on 'Judicial Child Care and Protection', pages 23-28; Netherlands Ministry of Justice: *Law and Motion 1990*, page 46, para. 3.2.5; and

Findlay, Colin, *Child   Abuse,   the   Dutch   Response,*   Child Abuse/International, Practice Magazine pages 374-381.

6. The European Convention on Human Rights: Council of Europe, Strasbourg 1987, Foreword and Article 5.

7. *Report of the Inquiry into the Removal of Children from Orkney in February 1991,* Edinburgh, HMSO 1992, paras. 6.1-70 and 15.2-3. (The Orkney Inquiry Report)

8. *McMichael v United Kingdom,* European Court of Human Rights 24.2.95 (51/1993/446/525).

9. Scottish Office: *Scotland's Children: Proposals for a Child Care Policy and Law* (CM2286), Edinburgh, HMSO, 1993 para. 6.17.

10. *Children and Young Persons Scotland,* Edinburgh, HMSO 1995, page 39, title. (The Kilbrandon Report)

11. *Report of the Inquiry into Child Care Policies in Fife,* Edinburgh, HMSO 1992, page 76, para. 11; page 125, para. 10; page 572, para. 3; and page 617, para. 8. (The Fife Inquiry Report)

114

Glossary
Terms Used in the Children's Panel System

Chairman of children's hearing
Each children's hearing has three panel members, one of whom is selected by the chairman of the children's panel as chairman for a particular children's hearing session. The chairman's responsibilities at a hearing principally relate to ensuring the proper conduct of the hearing.

Chairman of children's panel
The chairman of the children's panel is not only appointed as a panel member by the Secretary of State for Scotland, but as chairman of the children's panel of a local authority area. The chairman of the children's panel has specific responsibility to select or cause to be selected three panel members for a particular children's hearing. For that purpose the chairman has the responsibility to prepare or have prepared a rota of panel members to sit on children's hearings over a period of say three months at a time. By custom the chairman gives leadership to the panel members for his or her local authority area and represents the children's panel in discussion of national or local interests.

Child assessment order
In difficult circumstances where there was a reasonable suspicion of a child being ill-treated or neglected, the sheriff could grant an assessment order to allow for proper investigation.

Child protection order
In emergency care and protection situations if the sheriff is satisfied that the child is suffering or likely to suffer significant harm unless removed from the family the sheriff may issue a child protection order. A children's hearing would normally be arranged on the second working day to consider whether or not the order should be renewed. The hearing could do so but only for a limited period. A further hearing would have to be held by the eighth working day.

Children's hearing
The children's hearing is a lay tribunal consisting of three panel members, who are empowered to take decisions as to whether a child

115

requires compulsory supervision or not, and if so what type of supervision. An average hearing to consider a child's case would last approximately 40 minutes.

Children's panel
A children's panel is a group of persons in a Scottish local authority area appointed by the Secretary of State for Scotland with an interest in and concern for children to serve on children's hearings to consider cases of children referred to them by the children's reporter as being in need of compulsory supervision.

Children's panel advisory committee (C.P.A.C.)
The C.P.A.C. is a committee existing in a local authority area consisting of usually three persons appointed by the Secretary of State for Scotland and two councillors of the local authority. This committee is responsible for the selection of persons, whom they consider might be suitable as panel members, in order that the committee may recommend to the Secretary of State for Scotland that such persons be appointed as panel members. The committee would make similar recommendations regarding the reappointment of panel members. C.P.A.C.s have by custom taken an interest in the children's panel system in general.

Children's panel system
The children's panel system denotes the structure of welfare justice in Scotland inclusive of the children's panel, children's hearings, children's reporters, C.P.A.C.s and child care professionals concerned with the cases of children in trouble thought to be in need of compulsory supervision.

Children's reporter
The children's reporter to the children's panel receives reports on children thought to require compulsory supervision. The children's reporter assesses the evidence. If the children's reporter considers the child requires compulsory supervision the children's reporter refers the case to a children's hearing. The children's reporter may have to prove the grounds or allegation concerning a child in the sheriff court. The children's reporter could be described as a para-prosecutor.

Court of Session
The Court of Session is the highest civil court in Scotland. Case law emanates from the Court of Session in relation to appeals on points of

116

law on decisions of sheriffs in cases originating from children's hearings. A similar result may arise from appeals from sheriffs' decisions to the sheriff principal.

Discharge (of referral)

A children's hearing can discharge referral if they consider that the child does not require compulsory supervision. They may also do so if the grounds are denied by the child and/or parents, or the explanation of the grounds by the chairman of the hearing is not understood or able to be understood by the child. The sheriff can similarly discharge the grounds if the case is not proved by the children's reporter. If the family appeal against the children's hearing decision to the sheriff is successful, one of the options available to the sheriff is to discharge the grounds.

Exclusion order

An exclusion order would be granted by the sheriff in order to exclude the suspected abuser from the family home in the case of a child, who is alleged to have been abused by that person. It is better for the abuser to be removed from the family home rather than the child.

Family

In describing what occurs at a children's hearing, the word 'family' is used to denote the child and parents collectively present at the hearing.

Grounds

The word 'grounds' is an abbreviated form of 'grounds for referral'. Grounds denote reasons for a child being referred to the children's reporter or the children's hearing. The reasons relate to the trouble a child is in, for example, committing offences, truancy or being a victim of child abuse.

Juvenile panel

The Kilbrandon Report envisaged the juvenile panel as a lay tribunal of three ordinary persons from the local community to decide whether or not children required special measures of education or training on a compulsory basis. Later in legislation the juvenile panel became known as the children's hearing.

Kilbrandon Report

The government report 'Children and Young Persons (Scotland)' published in 1964 contained the consideration and conclusions of a committee, whose chairman was Lord Kilbrandon, a senior Scottish judge. The report became known as the 'Kilbrandon Report'. In 1964 this report presented radical proposals regarding Scottish justice for children in advocating the setting up of the children's panel system.

Legal aid
Children and their parents are entitled, if they so wish, to be legally represented both at children's hearings, the sheriff court and the Court of Session. In order to assist families who could not otherwise afford legal representation, monetary assistance known as legal aid is provided. However legal aid is not available to families for children's hearings.

Lord Advocate
The Lord Advocate is a government minister with special responsibility for public prosecution in the Scottish criminal courts. Prosecution of principally adult offenders is under the Lord Advocate's control. The Lord Advocate acts through the Crown Office in Edinburgh. The procurator fiscal is a local representative of the Lord Advocate.

Panel member
A panel member is a member of the children's panel. Three panel members form a children's hearing. There are over 1,500 panel members in Scotland.

Place of safety
A child may be taken to a place of safety in circumstances where the child is thought to have been abused or neglected, or at risk of abuse or neglect. A child may be arrested after committing offences and detained overnight by the police. In these circumstances the child may be taken to a place of safety. A place of safety is a place other than the child's own home. The home of a foster parent (carer), relative, children's home or residential school may be considered as a place of safety. The sheriff may and the hearing may renew a child protection order in order for the child to be taken or kept in a place of safety. Similarly the hearing can issue or renew a warrant to the same effect.

Proof
The word 'proof' is used in the context of the children's hearing directing the children's reporter to make an application to the sheriff to find the grounds of referral established in circumstances where the

grounds are denied by the child and/or parent, or where the child does not understand or is not able to understand the explanation of the grounds given by the chairman of the hearing. For the grounds to be established by the sheriff the children's reporter leads evidence in order to prove the grounds.

Referral
Referral is the act of reporting a child perhaps thought to be in need of compulsory supervision to the children's reporter, or in turn by the children's reporter to the children's hearing.

Review
The review of a supervision requirement occurs within a year of the making, continuing or varying of that requirement by a children's hearing. The review gives the children's hearing the opportunity to assess the child's progress or otherwise whilst subject to compulsory supervision, and to make an appropriate response as to continue, vary or terminate the supervision requirement.

Safeguarder
A safeguarder would be appointed by the children's hearing or the sheriff, if thought necessary, in the interests of the child. Thereafter the safeguarder so appointed would carry out an investigation of the child's case and provide a report to the hearing or the sheriff as the case may be. Safeguarders' reports have proved most helpful both to hearings and sheriffs. In the carrying out of their remit safeguarders in all but name act as children's advocates for the benefit of the welfare of children in particular difficulties.

Scottish Children Reporter Administration (S.C.R.A.)
S.C.R.A. is the national Scottish organisation within which children's reporters work. The Principal Reporter is the chief official of S.C.R.A.. Although nationally structured the work of children's reporters undertaken by S.C.R.A. is of necessity to focus the work of the children's reporter in relation to the local community and the children's panel of a local authority area.

Secretary of State for Scotland
The Secretary of State for Scotland is a government minister with overall responsibility for Scottish affairs in a number of government responsibilities, functions and interests, inclusive of the children's panel system.

Secure accommodation
Secure accommodation is lockfast accommodation within which a child may be liable to be detained. The use of secure accommodation is strictly controlled in terms of criteria whereby a child may be liable to be detained in secure accommodation. A children's hearing may make it as a condition of a supervision requirement or warrant that a child reside in residential care and be liable so to be detained.

Sheriff
In Scotland a sheriff is a local professional judge associated with the sheriff court. Within the children's panel system the sheriff hears proofs regarding grounds not admitted by the family at a children's hearing, or not understood by the child or unable to be understood by the child. The sheriff considers appeals by families against hearing decisions. In addition in emergency care and protection cases the sheriff may issue a child assessment, child protection or exclusion order.

Social education
The term 'social education' is referred to in the Kilbrandon report and is also synonymous with 'special measures of education and training'. Social education could be described as education in it's widest sense for a child in trouble. 'Social' emphasises the child's problems, whilst 'education' suggests possible solutions to these problems in a plan or programme of social work or other child care professional support for the child in trouble.

Supervision
Supervision is assistance or support given to a child and/or parent by a social worker to best help the child in trouble so that problems may be resolved. Supervision may be given either on a voluntary or compulsory basis. In the latter case the children's hearing would make a supervision requirement in respect of the child, insisting that the child be on compulsory supervision.

Supervision requirement
A supervision requirement is a document issued by a children's hearing requiring a child to be subject to compulsory supervision. The document will indicate what type of supervision. The child may be allowed to remain at home whilst the social worker gives appropriate

support to the family. Alternatively the child may be removed from home into foster or residential care.

Warrant

A warrant is a document issued by a children's hearing for a child to be taken and kept in a place of safety for a limited period, usually no more than 22 days at a time. The hearing can issue such warrants on 3 occasions up to a maximum of 66 days. The sheriff may grant a warrant on application by the children's reporter.

Bibliography: Scottish Children's Panel System and Related Matters

Asquith, S., *Children and Justice*. Edinburgh University Press, 1982.

Asquith, S. (ed.): 'Protecting Children: Cleveland to Orkney: More Lessons to Learn?', *Children in Scotland*. Edinburgh, HMSO, 1993.

Asquith, S. and Hill, M., *Justice for Children: Proceedings of an International Conference held in Glasgow 1992*. Martinus Nijhoff, Dordrecht 1994.

Burman, M. and Lloyd, S., *Police Specialist Units for the Investigation of Crimes of Violence Against Women and Children in Scotland: Department of Sociology*. University of Aberdeen: Scottish Office Central Research Unit Papers 1993.

Cleland, A. and Sutherland, E. (eds.), *Children's Rights in Scotland*. W. Green/Sweet and Maxwell, Edinburgh, 1996.

Cowperthwaite, D.J., *Emergence of the Scottish Children's Hearings System*. Institute of Criminal Justice, University of Southampton 1988.

English, J. and Martin, F.M., *Social Services in Scotland*. Scottish Academic Press 1988.

Fabb, J. and Guthrie, T. G., *Social Work and the Law in Scotland*. Butterworths, Edinburgh, 1992.

Report of the Inquiry Into Child Care Policies in Fife. Edinburgh HMSO, 1992. (Fife Inquiry Report):

Finlayson, A. F., *Reporters to Children's Panels: Their Role, Functions and Accountability*. Scottish Office, 1992.

Kearney, B., *Children's Hearings and the Sheriff Court*. Butterworths/Law Society of Scotland, 1987.

Children and Young Persons Scotland (1964). HMSO Edinburgh, 1995. (The Kilbrandon Report)

Lloyd, G. (ed.), *Chosen with Care?: Responses to Disturbing and Disruptive Behaviour (A Scottish Perspective)* Volume 2. Moray House Publications, 1992.

Lockyear, A. and Wilkinson, D., *Citizens Serving Children*. Scottish Office, 1992.

Martin, F.M., Fox, S. J. and Murray, K., *Children Out of Court*. Scottish Academic Press, 1981.

Martin, F.M. and Murray, K., *The Scottish Juvenile Justice System*. Scottish Academic Press, 1982.

Meek, R. *et al.*, *In the Child's Best Interests*. Scottish Child and Family Alliance, 1991.

Milne, R., *Who's Hearing*. Scottish Office, Edinburgh, HMSO, 1992.

Moore, G., *A Guide to Children's Hearings*. W. Green & Son, Edinburgh, 1989.

Murphy, J., *British Social Services: The Scottish Dimension*. Scottish Academic Press 1992.

Norrie, Kenneth McK., *Children (Scotland) Act 1995* (Greens Annotated Acts). W. Green/Sweet & Maxwell, Edinburgh, 1995.

Report of the Inquiry into the Removal of Children from Orkney in February 1991. Edinburgh, HMSO, 1992. (Orkney Inquiry Report)

Truancy and Indiscipline in Schools in Scotland. Edinburgh, HMSO, 1977. (The Pack Report)

Reid, D.H.S., *The Orkney Child Abuse Scandal: Suffer the Little Children.* Napier Press, St. Andrews, 1992 (for Miric).

Offenders aged 16 to 18: Report of a Working Party. Scottish Association for the Study of Delinquency, 1993.

Scottish Office (SWSG), *Compulsory Measures of Care for Children: Home Supervision.* Edinburgh, HMSO, 1989.

____ *Effective Intervention: Child Abuse.* Edinburgh, HMSO, 1989.

____ *Review of Child Care Law in Scotland.* Edinburgh, 1990.

____ *21 Years of Children's Hearings.* 1992.

Scottish Office, *Scotland's Children: Proposals for Child Care Policy and Law* (CM 2286). Edinburgh, HMSO, 1993.

____ *Scotland's Children: Speaking Out: Young People's Views on Child Care Law in Scotland.* Scottish Office, 1994.

Skinner, A., *Another Kind of Home: A Review of Residential Child Care.* Scottish Office, Edinburgh, HMSO, 1992.

Stone, F. (ed.)., *Child Abuse: A Scottish Experience.* British Agencies for Adoption and Fostering 1989.

Index

Sheriff Principal 48, 51, 59, 107, 117
  substitute own decision 29, 50
  warrant 27, 121
Social Work Department
  Child Protection Unit, *see* Child Protection Unit
  Social Work Department 68, 80
  social work practice 98-101
  social worker, *see* professionals
Social Work (Scotland) Act 1968 21, 70, 79, 107, 112
Spain 57
supervision
  compulsory care/supervision 24, 26, 27, 33, 40, 41, 45, 58-62, 67, 70, 80, 83, 87-93, 99, 101, 116-117, 119, 120
  foster parent (carer) 27, 98, 99, 101, 121
  supervision 27, 53, 61, 80, 90-93, 99, 101, 102, 111, 119, 120
  home supervision 27, 98, 99, 101, 120
  partnership 80, 91, 93

residential care/supervision 27, 61, 80, 90-93, 98, 99, 101, 102, 111, 121
review of supervision requirement 28, 49, 70, 89, 93, 119
secure accommodation (supervision) 28, 29, 53, 92, 120
stigma 98, 101
supervision/definition 79-81, 97, 120
supervision requirement 15, 27, 28, 29, 33, 120
voluntary /care supervision 26, 40, 79, 80, 87-93, 99, 101, 110
Switzerland 109, 110
tribunal, *see* children's hearing
UN Convention on the Rights of the Child 1989 15, 57-63, 103, 107, 110, 111
welfare 14-16, 49-51, 60, 77, 91, 103, 104
  welfare of child paramount 14, 59, 77, 83, 84, 101, 102
  welfare justice 13, 14, 116

Readers of *Introduction to the Scottish Children's Panel* may be interested in the following other youth justice publications from Waterside Press:

Introduction to
The Youth Court
incorporating 'The Sentence of the Youth Court'

Winston Gordon, Michael Watkins and Philip Cuddy

Produced under the auspices of the Justices' Clerks' Society, this handbook contains a straightforward outline of the youth court and current youth justice practice. It incorporates sections on sentencing which follow the successful format of *The Sentence of the Court: A Handbook for Magistrates* (published by Waterside Press in 1995). Direct mail price: £12.00 (add £1.50 p&p) (1996) ISBN 1 872 870 36 8

Juvenile Delinquents and Young People in Trouble in an Open Environment

Edited by **Willie McCarney**

An *international* survey of youth justice published in association with the International Association of Juvenile and Family Court Magistrates. Direct mail price £18 (add £1.50 p&p) (1996) ISBN 1 872 870 39 2

Growing Out of Crime

Andrew Rutherford

Undimmed by the 10 years since it was first published by Penguin in 1986, Andrew Rutherford's classic work about young people in trouble with the law. Direct mail price: £12.50 (add £1.50 p&p) (Second reprint 1996) ISBN 1 872 870 06 6

The Youth Court: One Year Onwards

Bryan Gibson *et al.*

Well received on publication, this practitioner level work (in contrast to the more basic treatment of the newer *Introduction to the Youth Court,* above) takes stock of the law and practice of youth courts in England and Wales eighteen months after their creation. Direct mail price: £15.00 (add £1.50 p&p) (1994) ISBN 1 872 870 14 7

All from Waterside Press, Domum Road, Winchester SO23 9NN
Tel or fax 01962 855567. E-mail INTERNET:106025.1020@compuserve.com